A multiplicity of "post-Christian" trends has, paradoxically, revived interest in the biblical image of man. It is no longer enough for the Christian to give formalized answers to the Nietzchean "Is God Dead?" He must convince modern man that the biblical divine-human relationship not only has current relevancy, but is the sole answer to the doubts and pessimism to which modern thinkers have systematically brought themselves.

This is the precise aim of Father Leo Scheffczyk in this little volume. Drawing the Christian image of man from a profound analysis of both the Old and the New Testament, the author then confronts this image with that to be found in leading modern philosophies and reflected in the literature of our day.

Man in the Old Testament regarded himself as a creature of God whose existence was menaced by the problems of life. The prototype of this man is Job, in whose life is evident the tragic history of Israel. Although heir to many of the evils which assailed Old Testament man, New Testament man is a creature redeemed and elevated to the level of sonship with God. The author brings this Christian image of man face-to-face with man as viewed by such philosophers as Lessing, Hegel, Feuerbach, Marx, Engels, Kierkegaard, Spengler, Klages, Gehlen, Jaspers, Sartre and Heidegger, and by such men of letters as Wolfe, Steinbeck, O'Neill, Hemingway, Mann, Dos Passos, Faulkner and Kafka. Scheffczyk shows that the modern image of man is fragmentary, yet offers some hope in that it shows man as directed toward the transcendental. And, Scheffczyk convincingly explains, Jesus Christ alone is the answer to the yearnings and the questions which beset these modern thinkers.

was born in Beuthen, attended the Univer- 38–1941 and pursued and theology at the from 1945–1947. In a Doctorate in Theology of Munich.

, Father Scheffczyk d as an assistant pro- logy. He is now a full Father Scheffczyk's le *A History of the ist,* published in Mu- historical study of rolingian period pub-

Scheffczyk have ap- European theological *en Theological Quar- r Theologische Zeit-*

Man's Search for Himself

MODERN AND BIBLICAL IMAGES

MAN'S SEARCH FOR HIMSELF
Modern and Biblical Images

by LEO SCHEFFCZYK

SHEED AND WARD : NEW YORK

Library of Congress Catalog Number: 66–22026 ✓

This book was originally published in German under the title, Der Moderne Mensch vor dem biblischen Menschenbild, © Verlag Herder KG Freiburg im Breisgau 1964.

Nihil obstat:
    Thomas J. Beary
    Censor Librorum

Imprimatur:
    ✠ Robert F. Joyce
    Bishop of Burlington
    June 2, 1966

The Nihil Obstat and Imprimatur are official declarations that a book or pamphlet is considered to be free of doctrinal or moral error. No implication is contained therein that those who have granted the Nihil Obstat and Imprimatur agree with the contents, opinions, or statements expressed.

Contents

5

❧ Introduction

The Modern Understanding of Man and the Task of the Christian

IT MAY NO LONGER BE SAID that contemporary man reflects less about himself than did man of earlier times. On the contrary, his sharpened sense of history enables him to scrutinize the depths of both spiritual and natural history. And, both because he feels an obligation toward the awesomely evolving world of which he is significant part and because the positive sciences have provided him with a vast knowledge about his own being, modern man feels capable of determining afresh his own place in that world and of defining his own nature more precisely; and he is determined to do so.

At the same time, modern man's determined effort to discover himself cannot be accompanied with that secure feeling of certitude which marked his self-discovery, in ages past, in the metaphysical order. The possibility of this certitude disappeared for modern man when he began to lose awareness of that metaphysical order with its absolutes. Inquiry, therefore, into the question of man and

9

his nature has undergone profound changes in our day. In recognizing that he has become an enigma to himself, modern man today faces his greatest intellectual challenge.

This enigma finds its outward expression in the fact that thought about man has fallen, almost universally, into a state of disunity. The departure from an absolute foundation which gave all created things their definite and circumscribed place in the cosmos as well as their clearly defined shape had to result in a disintegration of everything, including man's understanding of himself. The result is that today, even on the western cultural scene which is relatively restricted and held together by common history and origins, no homogeneous idea of man is any longer recognized by all as binding. Unity has given way to a confusing pluralism of views about man and life, and these views have only two features in common: all are oriented only to the world in which men find themselves; every supernatural yardstick for measuring what is truly human is banned in advance.

The result of this is the development of certain root-ideas concerning man and human reality which diverge so far from one another as actually to exclude one another. This certainly is the case in the relationship prevailing between Marxism and existentialism or between the pessimistic biologism of Spengler and the optimistic evolutionism of Teilhard de Chardin. One can hardly avoid the impression that, after relinquishing the one total conception of himself, man finds himself standing bewildered in the world, his hands full of bits and pieces.

However, since man is, at the same time, in need of spiritual unity and wholeness, his helpless situation leads him unknowingly to make absolutes out of the parts and to look upon those fragments he has rescued from the devastation as the whole for which he longs. Thus it happens that many of these fragmentary, substitute solutions are proposed as doctrines of true salvation. Moreover, they have a way of asserting their claims all the more insistently when they correspond less objectively to the whole reality of man and when their essentially fragmentary character is evident.

When exaggerated claims of this sort are realistically renounced, however, one has no choice but to acknowledge the disintegration itself as the only certainty on the human scene. This tendency has become particularly evident in certain achievements by modern artists. In the literary efforts of Gertrude Stein, for example, in the music of Arnold Schoenberg, or in the paintings of Pablo Picasso, the expressed intention is to demonstrate the fragmentary and disintegrated fact of reality by breaking down accepted continuities into senseless joinings of forms held together by pure association: the mirror of a reality in which all in collapsing, all is obliterated, and everything is tending toward isolation.

A similar artistic purpose was recently avowed by Wolfdietrich Schnurre in his novel, *Das Los unsrer Stadt*, where we read at one point:

In the dungeons of experience, the shoelace was found snagged in the campstove, the letter, crumpled up, was found lying under the lard barrel. . . . And so also do images come in through the cellar grates of the eyes: now this, now that . . . And therefore neither will I provide a coherence I do not have, neither will I falsify my rusty pennies into coins of gold. Truth is utterly without coherence.

The denial of coherence applies here not only to the outer reality, but also to man existing within that reality. This man has long since been attempting, first, to come to terms with the disintegration of his own image and of everything else, then to live with the chaotic fact of his own being as well as that of the world. In *Doppelleben* this has been expressed with brutal frankness by Gott-fried Benn whose work perhaps takes the most extreme position observed thus far in our bursting spiritual world. He says of the crumbling *I* of modern man:

Something is falling apart in this brain, something which was called "I" for four hundred years and which, as was so well suited to this period, preserved the human cosmos in trans-mittable forms for generations. And now this heritage has come to an end. . . . The line begun so magnificently as a sovereign life in *cogito ergo sum,* and hence anchored only in thought, is now coming in its own kingly image visibly to its end.

The judgment that man is coming to his end must be in-terpreted as meaning that he is "a half-successful being," that he is "a rough draft, a fling at being an eagle, but they have already torn his wings and feathers down."

A realistic observer of this situation will acknowledge the fact that these substitute solutions and fragmentary sketches do not really penetrate into the general consciousness of contemporary humanity, that they rarely attain to universal validity, and this alone hinders their multiplication considerably. Besides, these trumped-up root-images are generally one-sided. They betray themselves too soon in the game as abstract constructs lacking genuine contact with real man. As a consequence, they tend to gain currency only in restricted esoteric circles and in certain special provinces of the intellectual world. As an example here, we might consider the fate of the philosophy of existence which, in its approach and method, was ideally cut out for reaching and reshaping modern man wherever he might be found. Instead of pioneers of new human movements with far-reaching effects, however, its leading advocates are more often nothing more than founders of new sects regarded as authorities and luminaries by only an elite few. A true movement for humanity might be ascribed to communistic Marxism. Yet, even if we take seriously the power of ideology in general, we may honestly ask whether Marxism's effectiveness is not more properly attributable to a reckless use of physical strength than to the inner creative power of its ideas.

We should not be comforted, however, by the failure of modern anthropological conceptions to attain to universal influence. For even if they do not take hold of the whole of humanity and even if they do not, in their original coinage, gain currency with the majority of men, they nevertheless hold some influence over the universal consciousness by way of imperceptible germ notions and traces of ideas. It is not easy to make men into decided "atheists," committed "existentialists," or enlightened "humanists" who will identify themselves totally and consciously with the positions in question. Nonetheless, these positions are able to bring about an atmosphere in which the scales of values and the fundamental positions by which men live undergo unnoticeable changes—an atmosphere which permits disintegrating tendencies to move about, unperceived and anonymously.

To this we may add that even the most extreme ideologies, arising as they do from the problems of the times, can address themselves to the minds of the men of those times, and even gain partial acceptance. Thus, dialectical materialism in our age, appealing directly to man's social nature, really touches a nerve in his consciousness of the times in which he lives. Too, with the phenomenon of a shrinking world, men today feel a pressing need for human unity. The same may be said of humanism, because contemporary man, feeling himself called in a new way to maturity and self-reliance, finds a genuine attempt to answer his needs in the humanistic cult of freedom. Comparably, existentialism makes a powerful appeal to the self-consciousness of contemporary man with its pathos toward one's own unique existence. It is therefore understandable that man today, even if he does not subscribe fully to any of these positions, feels their substance running through his veins. For how can he fail to react to the undercurrent of their stimuli? Indeed, he responds like a perfectly tuned resonator.

Even though in their original forms these modern solutions to man's spiritual dilemma are not widespread, it does not mean that their general tendencies and appeals make no impression at all upon the general consciousness. In fact, they are able to touch even those persons who, standing firm in a classical understanding of man, attempt to isolate themselves totally. The possible influence of such new ideas is also increased—and even upon their opponents, we must remember—by the fact that there are no longer any truly isolated reaches in the spiritual and religious life of men. Because of that intensive and extensive communication among men that so typifies modern life, especially in the phenomenon of mass media, the germs of these new doctrines can penetrate everywhere, taking hold invisibly and encountering practically no resistance anywhere. Even in spiritual areas which actually oppose them openly, their quiet omnipresence can lead to unconscious but significant changes in thinking about man as well as to imperceptible but basic distortions of the good and the valid. Herein lies the real danger.

In the cases mentioned above, we were thinking of the immediate effects of the fragment-pictures of man upon the common consciousness and upon the still relatively private realms of the spirit. But there are also indirect influences traceable to this shattering of man's thinking about man. Though these may appear long after the breakdown itself, they can, nonetheless, attain to frightening dimensions.

One of the most serious after-effects of the obliterated human image is the pluralism of ideas about life and the world which pervades the entire spiritual scene today. This universal relativism threatens even those areas where absolute standards are still preserved. It is especially dangerous for persons of immature judgment and limited powers of distinction.

Where philosophies of existence and life become as varied as they have become in the pluralistic world of modern man, it is easy to assume that there is no single norm and idea of human existence that is binding for all men or that such a norm is at least *de facto* unknowable for man. Even if this impression does not actually cause one to yield his ground, it still hammers away at relativizing the idea of man according to which he lives his life, with the result that he comes to view his life as, at best, something determined by tradition, educational environment, or by some other personal factor, as something no longer unconditionally binding on himself or on anyone else. Hand in hand with this relativism, there often goes a sort of practical agnosticism with respect to the very recognizability of any absolute norms in things human; accompanying this agnosticism, in turn, is a certain distrust toward all claims to universal values and constants. Thus it seems that the shattering of man's image, even in areas which have remained relatively unassailable, can end up by undermining a man's entire spiritual foundation. And, in the final analysis, there must result some loss of that which was still recognized as binding in the image.

Even if it does not come to this, however, the image of man remains inwardly weakened, shaken, and outwardly unprotected when penetrated by relativism. This weakening often takes the form of indifferentism, so that indifferentism must also be considered as an indirect result of the shattering of man's image in modern times. To hold fast to an image of man regarded as true and binding requires that a person make a decision not simply once and for all, but repeatedly throughout the course of his life. It is only by virtue of this decision that one's idea of human reality takes on the definiteness, the clear contours and solidity it needs if it is to endure and to play any significant role in the shaping of one's life. But when the person allows the most variegated and alluring ideologies to pass before his eyes, with each such ideology displaying a certain affinity to his inwardmost bents and aspirations, the temptation quickly presents itself to avoid the decision and even to dally with the mutually exclusive possibilities at hand. At this point, the necessity of having to make a decision may no longer strike that person as particularly pressing, and indecisiveness may commend itself most seductively as an openness for everything and as the opportunity for a higher form of self-realization. For such indifferentism can always defend itself under the pretext that it is seeking a more personal, all-embracing, and, consequently, more integral humanity.

That such a danger is present even where, as in the Christian area, opposition is given to new ideologies, shows the readiness of many people of good faith to grasp and to hold fast to objectively irreconcilable philosophic positions. Such, for example, is the simultaneous embracing of an optimism which expects to see humanity fulfilled even in this world and of a tragic existentialism which sees man as determined hopelessly to foundering and ruin. Another example is the frequent and pathetic belief in the possibility of unifying the ideal of a democratic mass society with the aristocratic ethic of the free personality.

In the face of irreconcilable demands and claims, the refusal to make a decision will only occasion further negative effects, and even for that person who continues to resist the pressure of substitute solutions. The option to attempt to exist in mutually exclusive realms *at the same time* leads the person to a spiritual cleavage, to a form of existential schizophrenia. Something of this order is observable in all those cases where persons demonstrably act and live differently from the way they think and speak.

The critical observer of human behavior will note how this experience can arise in any number of situations today. Indeed, the impression is often given that people live their private lives with motives totally different (because drawn from totally different wellsprings) from those which they advocate and outwardly show. For one's neighbor and the outward realm in general, the highest ethical standards and ideals are held up as practically self-evident yardsticks; for the inward realm, however, the mediocre and half-way arrangement is allowed to prevail. Thus, while the world today appeals in exalted tones for perfect peace between nations, that same world hardly ever adverts to the truth that such peace can be achieved only as the fruit of incessant efforts for the pacification of one's own people, of one's own family—yes, even of one's own heart.

Great, too, is the longing for inner unity in an outwardly shrinking world. Yet, too little thought is given to how such inner unity can grow only from the virtues of selflessness and sacrifice, from overcoming private as well as national egotism. Demands for realization of the ideal of unity often go hand in hand with an utterly exhibitionistic egotism in the group as well as in the individual.

Nor does the danger of division spare the religious realm. Indeed, here it can grow to extraordinary dimensions. It is not only a question here of a disagreement between "Sunday Christianity" and "work-a-day heathenism." In our own day the split has assumed a different form, and it even divides those very "Sunday Christians" who actually are staunch in the faith and wish to live their lives by it, but who do not wish to admit that full Christian belief any longer pervades all their thinking, judging, feeling, and acting. In these people, then, only a part of the soul leads, as it were, an isolated spiritual existence. Furthermore, it is difficult to escape the impression that the average Christian's life is motivated and determined by values entirely different from those which are perhaps presupposed in his prayer or in which he concurs during the solemn moments of his ecclesiastical and liturgical experience.

The lack of courage to make decisions, when joined to the delusion of being able to live with contradictory demands, leads, in the religious area, to phenomena which were impossible before our time and which are often described in such terms as "silent apostasy," "paganism in the Church," extreme "situation ethics," "the mystique of sin," and the like. Together with all such we may include the heresy of spiritual pragmatism. No longer is spiritual pragmatism outwardly propagated as such; no longer does it fuss about itself, because ingenuously and without reflection it has long since been lived by those who call themselves Christians. As can be seen in all these cases, the shaping influence of a clear, well-delineated Christian picture of man has been lost, and indifferentism as well as relativism, as indirect effects of the modern disintegration of thinking about man, penetrate even into the Christian realm, threatening to deface the Christian conception of man.

The sober diagnosis of the situation which has emerged in modern times out of the shattering of the traditional picture of man results in what Max Scheler summed up more than a century ago, but which still has poignant validity today: "In the approximately 10,000 years of human history, ours is the first age in which man has become totally and thoroughly problematic for himself, in which he no longer knows what he is, but knows, however, that he does not know."

The problem is further compounded by the fact that the effects and after-effects of this intellectual disintegration fascinate also the consciousness of the young and penetrate even into the guarded reaches of the education and formation of youth. This cannot be avoided in a time when the personal significance of youthful existence is being accorded such widespread recognition, when, as a consequence, the difference between generations is divested of its absolute validity, when a rigid construction of authority is eclipsed by prosaic thoughts of partnership, and when the young live in so high a degree of communication with the adult world. In the light of these observations, it would be unrealistic to expect that the movements of the modern spirit would not address and stamp the thinking of the young. On the contrary, because of the high receptivity and plasticity of the young mind, because of its unsuspecting openness, and because of its ready impressionability especially eager for intriguing, dynamic ideas, it is no cause for surprise that the prevailing movements of our age should so easily affect our young people.

It is readily apparent, then, that all the various substitutes for an image of man anchored in the absolute do have considerable appeal to youth. For example, the worldly belief in progress, the humanistic passion for freedom, and the existentialistic defiance of existence will all have their fascination. At the same time, the phenomena of relativism, indifferentism, and the tendency to irrationalism—all of which appear in the wake of these modern influences—also display their insidious powers of attraction. Even if all these influences do not lead directly to those precisely formed attitudes which lack all semblance of the Christian ethic, they can still lead to unconscious preliminary decisions by dint of which the conscious decision for the Christian conception of man— a decision that is inevitable at a certain stage of development—becomes difficult and illusory.

In this situation the Christian who is conscious of his responsibilities to his times and his world—and here especially we have reference to the Christian educator in his particular calling to advocacy of religious truth—is burdened with an extremely difficult task. He is supposed to bring validity to the Christian truth about man for a world which, as far as the Christian message is concerned, has become a vast mission territory, and that same message is itself often splintered by contradictory points of view. He has the task of making Christian truth about man "edify" the Christian himself; in addition, he must so present Christian truth as to win over those who have turned to the new idols or who find themselves wavering between the fronts.

This broad educational work, the purpose of which is to lead man to a believing assent to the image of man as sketched by God himself and brought into reality in the human creature, implies a whole series of partial tasks which must be undertaken along the way. If decision is to be made in favor of Christian truth, two things are presupposed: a real difference between the false and the true; the capacity for distinguishing between them. This is what is meant by "distinguishing Christian things." For this reason, every Christian effort to comprehend what man is must, first of all, sharpen the vision for noting differences and peculiarities in reality. The contemporary man—especially the young who are influenced and sought on all sides in the ideology market and who are exposed to the most extreme influences—will be able, only by virtue of a sharpened vision, to put the various contradictory impressions in order, to separate the worthwhile from the worthless, to recognize the towering content in the Christian truth about man, and to decide himself in its favor.

Particularly necessary is this diacritical procedure when there are no limits placed upon either the exchange of ideas or their reciprocal influence, and when, as a consequence, more play is given to multiplicity of meaning in spiritual things and to a certain syncretism in one's thinking. Here also the religious man should always strive to see objectively how much of his scale of values, his ideas, drives, and his spiritual foundation is of purely worldly origin, lest purely natural drives (such as the ordinary will to live or, at the other extreme, the fear of existence) become the ruling powers within him. Where this critical control is not exercised, the full measure and beauty of the Christian image of man cannot clearly come into view (as is the case with the young) or else cannot be fully grasped (as is the case with adults).

This critical function must precede, as it must also always accompany, every effort to realize the Christian idea of man. However, it cannot even be practiced unless a man has at his disposal actual valid criteria for judgment which he can use responsibly. The propagation of such criteria must be considered as the second most important task if men are to acquire in their lives the Christian concept of man. The success of this particular educational effort is signalized by the formation of the conscience or at least by the formed awareness of values which must precede the actual functioning of the conscience. The more this spiritual attitude is opened to the world of the true and the good and the more it is experienced as one with the world and with God personally behind the universe, all the more precisely will man be able to measure the phenomena in the reality about him according to truth and falsehood, goodness and evil, the worthwhile and the worthless. The deciding yardstick, then, will be the natural conformity of things to the absolutely good and true, which is to say their likeness to God. By using this yardstick, it will be possible for the individual to see in advance the inadequacy of materialistic, positivistic, existentialistic, and purely humanistic conceptions of man and to recognize how inferior they are to a religious conception of man.

Since, however, the Christian picture of man is not a creation of natural powers and not even the fruit of a purely natural religion, natural yardsticks will not suffice for understanding it and for making a decision about accepting it. This difficulty makes it essential that, in defining natural standards, every educational effort be made to open up the vision for the transcendental, that dimension of the divine and the mysterious which, though not readily at man's disposal, is a matter of grace. But this opening of the mind for that note of "absolute otherness" which is contained in the revealed conception of man is no longer a natural pedagogical activity proper to the educator; it can be effected only in the specific material of Revelation itself, that is, only in personal contact with its witnesses and its living testimony.

At this point, the search for the Christian idea of man takes us to Holy Scripture both as to the authority from which the final supernatural yardstick is to be taken and also as to the source of positive motives for deciding in favor of the God-willed, God-revealed conception of man. For it should be borne in mind that the preceding critical activity is only preparatory in nature and that, since it goes no further than distinguishing the true from the false, it can serve only to lead the individual to the threshold of commitment to the one and only true conception of man. This commitment neither can be made on purely rational grounds in a syllogistic process nor can it be forced with irrational drives. By its nature, this commitment can come about only in an area of freedom pre-enlightened by those motives by which men are wont to be moved.

The extremes which are, at the very least, possible as a

result of forcing assent with a claim to scientific validity
or with the use of outward authority and power may be
seen in the Soviet educational experiment (particularly
in the German sphere of Soviet influence), the negative
lessons of which cannot here be passed over. Shored up,
as they are, with intellectual respectability and maintained with force, such doctrines still lead directly to
inner resistance and to total rejection, especially among
young people. But this rejection of a pretension to the
absolute that is recognized as forced (and, therefore, untrue) does not necessarily open the mind positively to
what is really true and to what is genuinely absolute. In
many cases the contrary is true: the instinctive rejection
of an arbitrarily enforced claim to the truth turns to a
disbelief regarding the very existence of truth and absolutes in general. This may serve as a warning sign for
those engaged in communicating Christian truth, a
process which should always take realistically generous
cognizance of the strong sense of freedom in modern man.

Therefore, the option for the conception of man taught
by God in Revelation and declared as binding can be
brought about only by confronting man freely with the
testimony of this Revelation and with its intrinsic per-
suasive power. At this point the Christian proclamation of
the Gospel as well as Christian education (which, in this
connection, is no longer restricted to the mere function
of communicating knowledge, but must be a personal witnessing and proclamation of the truths contained in God's
Revelation) have the task of bringing to man God's Word

concerning man in its full form. In this way will man be able to comprehend the "breadth and length and height and depth and to know Christ's love which surpasses knowledge" (Ephesians 3, 18 f.).

The proclaimer of the Word may have every confidence that this divine Word, if witness be borne to it in its unqualified integrity, is, in itself, a power which "shall not return void" (Isaia 55, 11); indeed, it is a power if the work of the proclaimer is not to be pervaded by subtle insecurity and, therefore, inwardly broken in advance. The proclaimer of the Word must always be optimistic that his work will prevail and reach the man of today in spite of all appearances to the contrary; he must be confident that that Word still means more to man today than all the fascinations and ideologies of the modern world. Moreover, the experiences which give the proclaimer of the Word graphic knowledge of the difficulty of his task teaches him also the opposite, namely, that a living confrontation with the fullness of the truth of Scripture also makes its impression upon modern man. Especially is this so if modern man can be brought to an awareness that all of Scripture is much richer in content than is suspected on hearing those commonplace, superficial expressions of it which are seldom more than a few clever phrases and generalizations.

At this point the proclaimer of the Word should, first of all, let Holy Scripture speak for and bear witness to itself. He should let the Scriptures bring out their own inner meaning and let them teach the hearer to see both

how overflowing they are with human truth and what a
treasure of anthropological thought they contain. In this
first stage the Scriptures should be brought out of themselves to enlighten the listener and in full confidence that
their light can also penetrate where our human judgment
tells us there are only drawn blinds and locked doors.

For modern, history-oriented man it will also be helpful
to explain how the revealed truth about man, expressed
in Holy Scripture, is unfolded before man, step by definite
step, leading to a clear culmination. In the light of this
divine pedagogy—witness, in the concrete, the inner connection between the Old Testament and the New—modern man can come to see that the truth and teaching
about man in Revelation is itself a living organism which
grew from small beginnings and in which is hidden an
argument for its authenticity and its independence from
human construction and invention. The knowledge of this
organic development will always convey to him some
understanding of how God always adapts himself to
human powers of comprehension at any given time, how
God, in this reference, always deals "humanly" with men,
and how God at all times gives full consideration to man's
historical situation and composure. And so it is important
for the present state of the hearer that he be brought to
see that his current situation also stands under a divine
reckoning and is a critical moment in the biblical sense.
For the divine call to the truth addresses man in such a
way that he sees his own existence in a new light; in this
light man will see that he must give a fitting response.

In order that the fullness of scriptural truth receive its truly objective value, however, its proclaimer must take care also that the basic ideas and judgments in Holy Scripture are stated in their original purity and not so distorted by false preconceptions as to frustrate the effect of their original power. This means that Scripture's proclaimers must be able to liberate those notions from various atrophies and encrustations which, as a result of man's conceit and misunderstanding, may have set in ever since God first began shouldering man with the task of propagating divine truth. For example, such notions as "flesh," "soul," "heart," "spirit," "life," and the like, essential for biblical anthropology, can no longer be brought home to modern man without a conscious effort to reconstruct their original meanings; otherwise they will be understood in terms of a later dualism which is neither at all biblical nor corresponds any longer to how most men view things today. For modern man is again trying to see human nature as a unit. No longer is he overly concerned with the structure of the various essential parts or with the differences among them; on the contrary, man is once again deeply interested in the knowledge of man as an entity whole in himself and, in some cases, as an entity before God. Here, then, the interpreter of Holy Scripture will make the surprising observation that genuine biblical thinking corresponds remarkably with modern man's understanding and interpretation of life. The reason for this is that the biblical sense of the world was not world-contained, static, and ontological (like that of the ancient

Greek world or of the Middle Ages which followed); rather, it was definitely opened to the idea of transcendence and was dynamic and action-oriented. But these are properties which are also proper to the dynamic and transcendental universalism of modern thought.

At this point, the proclaimer of the biblical testimony about man—testimony which, first of all, ought to bring out the true meaning of Scripture through an unprejudiced use of modern biblical exegesis—must turn his attention to a task that seems almost irreconcilable with this primary task. The mere communication and exposition of Scripture through repetition of the biblical words will always remain the same sterile, inbred biblicism it has always been. A living proclamation of Scripture, forthrightly addressed to modern man, must also state the biblical truth in such a way that it can be understood and examined as a proposition charged with the reality of the present moment. The proclaimer of divine truth must also be conscious of the fact that the Word of God must ever be made to live vibrantly as a new historical phenomenon for man. It must be set before man in a form which is proper to the times and which respectably commends itself to his intelligence and imagination. It simply will not do to repeat the Bible's words and to think that an exact reproduction of its supposedly timeless contents will necessarily win for it the respectful attention of men of this age. The vocation to announce biblical truth must, therefore, be marked with a zeal to translate biblical truths into the terms of contemporary man if these men are to be expected to recognize this Word as something relevant to life as they know it and live it. A living communication and acceptance of scriptural truth can succeed only when the pastor or educator is determined to speak in the categories and terms understood today and to fit the old truths into current conceptions of the world. "Thus he must dare to understand the Word of yesterday as a Word of today" and to speak it as such, for it will be understood and, indeed, understandable only as a Word of today. This demands from the modern proclaimer the effort and courage to restate the biblical truth about man in a language which expresses modern feeling and thinking. To measure contemporary religious statements against this ideal will enable the proclaimer to see, without underestimating the difficulties in fulfilling the ideal, how much still remains to be done in this area. On the whole, the impression cannot be avoided that the language in which biblical truth is usually explained is quite alien to the way modern man thinks and judges. Too often biblical expression is unsuited for fruitful understanding by the young, and its frequently bypasses, practically unnoticed, the understanding of men in general. We shall succeed in removing this unfortunate obstacle once we begin really to integrate central biblical ideas and judgments with those emotional and existential overtones that mark contemporary thought. For example, the notion of "grace," which simply cannot be exchanged for an entirely new notion, could be so expressed that it signifies not only an objective supernatural good, but also so that it includes

the loving movement of God toward man, a movement
which elicits from man a corresponding movement toward God. As a matter of fact, this explanation would
restore to use one of the oldest biblical understandings of
grace, one which, incidentally, has been all but lost.
Similarly, the idea of "sin" might be expressed in such a
way that the existential distorting of one's own being
and the loss of self also come through as decisive and
essential to sin. The reality of salvation, as it emerges in
Holy Scripture, should be made more unmistakably recog-
nizable as an event which really involves man and which
takes place within man; further, the "theological" significance of Holy Scripture's "anthropological" content
should be made significantly clear.

It must not be overlooked here that the interpretation
and "translation" of central scriptural ideas for the modern
mind can also present problems. Translating the biblical
message into the language of modern man can lead to a
loss of substance and to a falsification of the original
meaning and intent. But this danger can be set aside,
first of all, if the biblical testimony is validated against
the Church as the authentic interpretative authority and,
secondly, if, as the Scriptures themselves urge, we
"test all things [and] hold fast that which is good" (1
Thessalonians 5, 21). If, then, in our Christian efforts we
keep simultaneously in view the norms of Revelation and
the spirit of the times, if we seek to penetrate deeper into
both, and if, furthermore, we do not shy from advocating
the scandal of Revelation against the false demands of

the world and the times, then our religious proposals will not fail to strike and to hold to the middle way among extreme philosophies of the day.

Accordingly it is necessary that the Christian be familiar with the utterances and professed understanding of the modern spirit, that he know and understand the various ideologies of his time in their deeper implications, and that he grasp the kernels of truth they contain. Only in this way will he be able to conquer them from within and so bring about their positive incorporation into the Christian idea of man.

On the one hand, the advocate of Christian thought may be confident that there are germs of truth even in the most remote areas of human thought, because the human spirit cannot, even in a conscious departure from divine truth, cease to be stamped by that very Truth to which it still must bear witness, even unwillingly. On the other hand, he may set out from the "divine *a priori*" that the truth of Revelation is the principle of the whole, containing within itself all human truths and fulfilling them perfectly. From such a grace-oriented and optimistic fundamental attitude in the proclamation of scriptural truth pure and solid conviction is bound to flow. For this is no longer the sort of impatient apologetics that sought merely to guard its own ancient possessions, exhausting itself in the denial of what it opposed, because what it opposed happened to be new. Where there is a sincere will and a genuine ability to integrate all positive manifestations of human truth, the unprejudiced man will receive a vivid impression of the universality of the Christian proposal. And the conviction will begin to grow that man, as understood in Revelation—because of a universality into which all creatural values are fitted from the very start, a wholeness within which even new and fashionable things find their places—is the only man that is really "new" and true to the times. In this way it becomes possible both to experience the novelty of Christian reality, so necessary precisely for the young, and, at the same time, to be truly faithful to the "old and the true." And such an experience could easily make the "ins" and "outs" of fad and fashion seem very much "passé," "obsolete," and "out of date" even for the young.

This positive and open approach in the struggle with modern ideologies will therefore take special care to point out where the fragmentary character of their preliminary assumptions shows through, where the splintered edges of their views of reality can be seen. Only in this way will our positive approach be able to show how tangibly— precisely in these broken lines—the fragments fit into the larger unity of the revealed picture of man. To the extent that such a proclamation of Christian truth is prepared to regard adverse proposals as legitimate questions and to acknowledge their positive significance, it is thereby declaring its preparedness to subject itself and its own standpoint to the questioning of the other side, its willingness to seek a reconciliation of differences, and to define its own peculiarities as the peculiarities they are. Thus the necessary conflict can also take the form of a living discussion that opens up new funds of knowledge on all sides.

The basic optimism which should characterize the Christian in discussions with modern thinkers and advocates of substitute religions must not be confused with optimism regarding the success of his efforts. Such an attitude would be unrealistic. It would mean underestimating the subjective power and fascination of the non-Christian ideologies and a failure to recognize the fact that a testimony to belief cannot be forced from someone who has been addressed with the imperative of a logical syllogism. There is no human guarantee of success of revealed truth purely on the strength of its being proclaimed. However, authentic proclamation of Revelation will never be without some efficacy, for it will at least always strengthen Christians in their belief.

In keeping with these briefly sketched principles, the following chapters will attempt to extract from the Bible the idea of man it contains and to confront modern substitute solutions with that idea. The conclusion should follow that the idea of man encountered in Revelation commends itself most respectably to the present world and that the sound of the divine utterances about man also have their clear echo in men today, even when those utterances seem to be spoken in a desert. Because our emphasis is placed on gaining understanding of the Bible as a source and norm for thinking about man, the major part of our work here will be dedicated to an investigation of Holy Scripture itself. A caution here may be needless that our presentation of the biblical idea of man is not to be regarded as a substitute for a thorough and detailed theology of man. We shall restrict ourselves to proposing several decisive truths from both the Old and the New Testament and, by examining the inner dimensions of these truths, we shall endeavor to establish the existence of useful ties between the biblical idea of man and contemporary anthropological thought.

1

The Message of the Old Testament:
Man Face to Face with God

A. THE CREATURE OF GOD

The first feeling one may experience in searching through the record of the Old Testament for its statements about man is disappointment; the search is apparently fruitless. This is understandable, and disappointment will give place to enthusiasm once it is understood that divine Revelation is to be regarded as God's way of making *Himself* known and accessible to the world. God not man, is the true center of Revelation, its real object; only incidentally is Revelation theoretical doctrine about man.

Accordingly, what on first blush seems to be an incompleteness in the Old Testament record is, in actuality, a decidedly positive feature in scriptural teaching regarding man. Holy Scripture does not regard man merely as a being in himself, as an essentially autonomous and distinct entity; man, rather, is seen only as absolutely dependent upon and related to his God. We must look, therefore, to God's statements about His own orientation to the world and about His dealings with creation if we are to uncover what He will tell us about man. In the Old Testament we encounter man only "in parentheses," mentioned only incidentally in passages about the personal God. Accordingly, "man" constitutes no independent theme in the Old Testament, no subject that could be treated in itself. To study man, therefore, in the Old Testament record is best done by turning our attention to the theme of "God and man."

The Old Testament offers little by way of an ontological, or philosophical, definition of man as a being among other beings. Since Old Testament man is generally found together with his God, we must take a theological approach and restrict our interest in man to the specifically religious aspects which constitute the strength of the Old Testament idea. In this view of man, the deepest consideration is the fact of his *being created* by God, of his being a living *creature*.

Before examining the Old Testament any further, we should here preface our study with an understanding that the picture of man we shall discover is not going to be, at first, a picture of a concrete, individual man. The Old Testament has not yet discovered the individual, the "human personality," as such. The discovery of the individual man was delayed until the time of the prophet Jeremiah. On the whole, the Old Testament understands the term "man" as a generality, as human existence not yet separated or isolated from the all-embracing collectivity. Although, in this respect, the picture of man would seem to be incomplete, we shall shortly observe that we are observing distinctive features of man, since unity and community life are regarded here as highly significant human qualities.

The first characteristic of man in the Old Testament is that he is essentially the creation of another and higher Being. Because we have grown up familiar with this fact in our religious thinking, today we tend to regard it—and unfortunately so—as a purely formal and external presupposition regarding humanity, not to be taken very seriously in itself or even in the Israelitic conception of the world and man. Yet this fact has a significance for Israel that cannot be overestimated, especially against the background of the surrounding pagan world.

In the Babylonian creation-myth of Enuma Elish, man comes into being in the wake of an awesome theomachy between the gods and the powers of chaos. Out of the dismembered corpse of Tiamat (the principle of the original sea of chaos) the powerful god Marduk creates heaven and earth; but it is out of the blood of the slain Kingu, Tiamat's husband, that Marduk forms the human race. Accordingly, man takes his origin out of divine substance and is, in the very beginning, a part of a divine union. From this account, human essence appears to enjoy a dignity equal with divinity's. However, on reflecting that the gods themselves are only parts of one and the same natural reality, it then becomes clear that man's apparent exaltation proves to be only an expression of his deep imprisonment in the cosmic powers.

How different, in comparison, is Israel's consciousness of man as a creature! Although in the biblical account of creation traces of myths are present (these are used, however, only for making the message more graphic), yet the God of Israel stands as all-powerful Lord and sovereign Creator over the world and men. The sovereignty with which God simply and effortlessly creates the universe in the power of His Word is an expression of His absolute transcendence even over man.

Implied here is God's infinite supremacy and His absolute power to dispose of man as He wills. In the knowledge that he has been created by God, man is conscious also of a radical dependence upon his Creator. This means for man that he does not possess the basis and origin of his own being, that he is, from every consideration, related to the absolute God, that he is nothing when he stands on his own. The Old Testament sets this sobering view of man, the creature, before our eyes on every page, but it does so with unforgettable relevancy in the Yahwistic account of creation wherein man is portrayed as made out of the earth (Genesis 2, f.), when it describes man as dust and ashes comparable in his transitoriness to plants (Psalms 90, 6) and animals (Ecclesiastes 3, 19).

Of course it would be a mistake were we to regard this as the one and only possible aspect of man's creaturality. The Old Testament takes a basically dialectical approach to creaturality, opposing the negative factors immediately with positive considerations. For example, man's radical dependence upon God is regarded at once as man's grand liberation from the world, from the fear of the world and the cosmic powers which constituted the real source of mythical thinking. By viewing himself as a creature wholly dependent upon God, man was able to free himself from acknowledging dependence upon anything else; at the same time, his thinking about his Creator and everything implied in that aspect of God filled man with new confidence and security. Therefore, how perfectly logical for Israel, conscious of its radical dependence upon the Creator, to praise Him without ceasing and to designate the very fact of creation as an occasion for a continuing hymn of praise.

The very positive and uplifting quality in Israel's view of creation is ultimately due to the fact that its conception of the absolute creatorhood of the transcendent God was intimately bound to its knowledge of the gracious affection of God for His works, and especially for man. It would be impossible to come to such understanding from mythical accounts of man's origin, because the Maker has no deep affection for His works according to those world views which regard man either as coming into being out of the disintegration of the original divine body or —as in many gnostic myths—as a chance by-product in a battle of the gods. The demiurge of myth has no inner relationship with what he has made; there is no communication between man and such a world-maker. Where the material world is thought of as coming into being as the droppings or refuse of a higher spiritual state, that "creating" god can regard his creation only with disdain and rejection.

On the other hand, the thought of so exalted and

transcendent a Creator as is Israel's God implies affection
and concern on the part of God for His work. To be a
creature offers the consolation of being wanted and
showered with gifts by God, of being the object of divine
thoughts and goodness. For this reason, in the biblical
account of creation reference to God's goodness is repeated so often in the expression, "and God saw that it
was good." Actually, it was this recognition of divine
goodness that originally brought Israel into communication with the Creator, a relationship that was to mark
Israel's future. To have been "created" in this Old Testament sense is not at all the same thing as being hopelessly
remote from God and, as it were, banned into exile. On
the part of God, it is an act of gracious affection for man;
on the part of man, to have been created means a most
profound relationship to God as the cause and preserver
of man's being. But the Old Testament developed its own
understanding of the reality of this relationship contained
in the idea of creation, and this understanding leads us
more deeply into its religious or theological anthropology.

B. THE GOD-RELATED BEING

The idea of creation lies behind the idea of any lasting
relationship between man and God, and the thought of
the Old Testament bears this out. That man is essentially
a God-related being is brought out with equal clarity
throughout the Old Testament in the idea of the *Godless
existence* of man. The Old Testament, it has often been

pointed out, never knew the phenomenon of godlessness in the sense of a positive, theological denial of God. Of course, there were the mockers who ridiculed the God-fearing man (Psalms 1, 1) and who exalted themselves over Him; there was the fool who said in his heart: "there is no God" (Psalms 53, 2); then there was the unjust man who acted as if God did not exist (Psalms 10, 4; 14, 1; 53, 2); and, of course, the idolator who exchanges the true image of God for false gods and then throws the moral demands of God to the winds (Isaia 2, 8–20; Jeremia 2, 11; 7, 17 f.; Osee 4, 13; 6, 6). Nevertheless, there is no man throughout the Old Testament who is godless in the sense of expressing outright disbelief in the existence of God, no man who holds to a world without God. The "disbelief" of the Old Testament man is, then, nothing more than a degenerated belief in God, a belief which actually pre-supposes and even recognizes God's existence even while failing to respect Him in practice.

If we now turn our attention to the actual event of crea-tion, man's essential relatedness to God becomes even more understandable. Clothed in schematic and poetic ex-pressions, the first account of creation was not intended to give Israel cosmological knowledge concerning the begin-nings of world history, although the author of this account allows much cosmological detail from his own conception of the world to find its way into his depiction. His deepest concern was relating the Israelitic belief in divine elec-tion and the Covenant back to the very beginning of all history. This author was writing at a time when the peo-

ple Israel had conceived as a living reality the thought of
its singular election from among all peoples for divine
guidance and dispensations. From this standpoint it was
necessary for this author to show that the choosing and
redeeming God was none other than the Creator Himself,
so that the election of Israel and the Covenant appear
as already planned in the pre-historical moments of creation. But just as Israel, with the establishing of the Covenant, exists as a people elevated by Yahweh to the dignity
of partnership, so also does man (Adam is, at once, both
the one and only individual man as well as all humanity)
appear as God's partner in the work of the historical realization of divine plans in the world. The account of
creation leaves no doubt in the reader's mind that man is
the one and only creature standing *immediately* before
God. The creation account recognizes also, in a "genuinely humanistic" manner, that all other created things
were made for the sake of man so that he may use and
dispose of them as he wills (Genesis 1, 28). Yet, at the
same time, it is made eminently clear that man is not a
law unto himself, that man's power over the rest of
creation was never intended for his own glorification.
Positively stated, all created beings are intended, medi-
ately or immediately, to serve the single, absolute purpose
of God's glory.

To signify both the truth of man's creation-linked relatedness to God and his appointment as God's partner
in the work of history, the Old Testament uses an expression which is absolutely fundamental for our inquiry

concerning the biblical conception of man: "our [God's] image and likeness" (Genesis 1, 26). These words are used, even in the very first pages of Holy Scripture, to describe man's relatedness to God. Even though the full text of Genesis, at this point, has not been fully explained, even though exegetes have felt it necessary to make further investigations (which, in turn, have led to a multiplicity of interpretations), there can still be no doubt that these four words, spoken in direct connection with the creation of man and invested with a very definite note of solemnity, constitute an enormously important statement about man. Even if the surrounding text does not explain the expression, "Let us make mankind in our image and likeness," and regards more, as if essentials, the *implications* in man's being the image of his God, it is nevertheless clear that the unique dignity of man's relatedness to God is intended and expressed (*cf.* Genesis 2, 7; 9, 6). The author of the Genesis text clearly sees man as a king in the midst of all God's creatures (Genesis 1, 28; Sirach 17, 3), as a representative of God in the world, standing and acting in His place.

The words of the eighth Psalm concerning the majesty of man have always been regarded as fulfillment of the words of Genesis, even though that psalm (8, 6-9) does not use the expression, "image and likeness." But what it does say about man's place before God as being "a little below the angels" and about God's "crowning him with glory [*kabod*] and honor [*hadar*]" may be taken as a sort of commentary on the fundamental statement in the

Genesis account of creation. The eighth psalm tells us that "likeness" to God is an ineradicable distinction belonging to man, who comes from God, who acts as His mandated and official emissary in the world, and who refers all onlookers back to God. At the same time, the words of the psalm make clear also that the distinction proper and unique to man is to be understood dialectically: it refers to man's *relative* size and thereby indicates the limitations in man's place before God. For the fact that man is only a *little* below Elohim is a reference to his stature as the image of God, while the fact that he stands *below* Elohim (and is, therefore, only a copy, so to speak) indicates the finiteness of man's essence.

We may again experience a certain disappointment here. In comparison with later theology, which went so much farther in mining the wealth of implications in man's being made in the "image and likeness" of God, the Old Testament is quite sparse. Nor do the later books of the Old Testament provide even occasional elaborations of the idea. For what the book of Wisdom (2, 23) and that of Ecclesiasticus (17, 3) say of man's likeness to God is but an insignificant extension of what was already said in Genesis (Ecclesiasticus referring to the ethical obligation of man who is the "image" of God; Wisdom referring to deathlessness as an intrinsic note of "likeness" to God). We might explain this apparent deficiency with any one of a variety of reasons, such as the fact that the Old Testament (and also the New Testament) does not

propose or seek to propose systematic doctrine at all, so
that its contents do not unfold logically.

On a more fundamental level, however, this lack of data
about man's likeness to God has another explanation
which points significantly to the grand framework of human salvation-history. It can be stated (as many have
so stated since Irenaeus of Lyons first formulated the
thought) that the Old Testament could not fully develop
the truth of man's likeness to God because the perfect
human image of God had not yet been realized. "In
earlier times," wrote Irenaeus in *Adversus Haereses*, "it
was said that man was made in the image of God, but
it was not demonstrated. For the Logos was still invisible."
Thus, for Irenaeus, the true image of God is the Logos-
become-man, which causes Irenaeus to state further that
"the image of God is the Son according to whose image
man was made. This is why the former appeared in the
fullness of time, in order to make clear how similar the
copy is to the original."

In the light of this salvation-history interpretation of the
divine likeness (which is fully realized only in the Son
of God-become-man), the apparently defective Old Testament data immediately take on greater meaning and significance. What, therefore, at first appeared to be a deficiency and a gap in coherence regarding the truth of
man's likeness to God is, in reality, only the space, the
opening for that place which the God-man, Jesus Christ,
will one day fill as the *perfect* likeness of God. The Old
Testament information is, therefore and in that sense,

necessarily incomplete. From the very beginning, space is left for something new, and in such a way that, even in its absence, it is already somehow present.

C. THE VERBAL-DIALOGICAL EXISTENCE

When we refer to man's being as relatedness to God, we are, of course, speaking in those static, objective categories reserved for mere things and hardly proper for the general behavior of persons with one another or for the particular quality of Old Testament thought. Biblical man's conception of the world is dynamically active because of his living experience both of God's infinite remoteness and, at the same time, His immediate proximity. Here our thinking must constantly go beyond itself up to God's infinity and then return back to the consciousness of His unimaginable nearness. Thus man's relatedness to God must be expressed in a dynamic and personal way if we wish it to approximate the reality experienced by the man of the Bible.

Naturally enough, the Old Testament itself seeks to approximate that experience with the notion and reality of the *Word*. For the Word constitutes that dynamic dimension which stands between God's infinite transcendence and His nearness to the world, which expresses the union of God and the world as well as their distance from one another.

For this reason, *creation by the utterance of the Word* is an essential quality in the Old Testament idea of creation. The great difference between biblical and mythological ideas of creation can be noted very clearly in this matter of creating with words. For "making in the word" signifies the powerful composition of being and purpose in such a way that the created being, like the expression of a thought, remains with the speaker while also truly departing from him and henceforward existing in relative independence. From this we come again to that unity of remoteness and proximity of God regarding the creature, a unity impossible in creation-myth accounts.

Now in the Old Testament faith, every outward act of God is the work of his word, whether it be the original creation (Genesis 1) or the subsequent preservation of the world (Psalms 147, 15 ff.), the revelation made to the prophets (1 Samuel 9, 27), or the Law given to His people. The creative power of this word is a fundamental idea in the Old Testament and is expressed in its texts with extreme frequency. The prophet Isaia states it with striking clarity:

For just as from the heavens the rain and snow come down and do not return there till they have watered the earth, making it fertile and fruitful, giving seed to him who sows and bread to him who eats; so shall my word be that goes forth from my mouth; it shall not return to me void, but shall do my will, achieving the end for which I sent it (Isaia 55, 10–11).

Just as we can conclude from the account of creation that, because all things came into being by the power of God's word, all the created things of the universe possess thereby a verbal quality and have likewise been "worded,"[13] so, in a similar way, the above-quoted text of the prophet Isaia communicates still another truth which is essential to the biblical understanding of the word: the word is invested with a reflected power which declares that the word must radiate back to its author. It does not remain locked up within itself; rather it emits a reflection which returns to its point of origin. This and nothing else is meant by the prophet's statement that every word of Yahweh is intended to return to Him, "achieving the end" for which it was sent. Accordingly, the word in the Old Testament is a ray of light which takes such shape in the world that it becomes a mirror of itself and can then be reflected back to its origin. How effectively the Old Testament sees this "answering character" in all created things, even lifeless creatures, is shown with striking vividness in those hymn-like passages where nature appears empowered to sing the praises of God and where their simple existence is regarded as a praising response to the greatness of the Creator.

Listen to the immensely impressive nineteenth psalm (2–5):

The heavens declare the glory of God, and the firmament proclaims his handiwork. Day pours out the word to day, and night to night imparts knowledge; not a word nor a discourse whose voice is not heard; through all the earth their voice resounds, and to the ends of the world, their message.

The existence and beauty of the heavens are understood here as an answer which goes out from them and out beyond the world to the Creator.

The man of the Bible can, therefore, formally summon even the lifeless things of the earth to praise God and return to Him the honor He placed in them. Such is certainly the import of the "Hymn of the Three Young Men" (Daniel 3, 57 ff.): "Bless the Lord, all you works of the Lord, praise and exalt him above all forever." Whereupon all creation and its orders pass in review, so that each and every creature can join, as with one voice, in the praising of God.

Statements of such biblical truths regarding lifeless creation are not to be diluted by recalling the anthropomorphic and allegorical manner of thinking encountered in the Old Testament. The meaning here is unequivocally evident: merely by their existence, the things of nature should, can, and do fulfill a function which approaches a response to the love of God in creating, even though their response is not through human speech.

In the Old Testament, conscious and formal expression of the response to God is reserved to man alone. Originating from a particularly solemn and exalted word of God ("Let us make mankind in our image and likeness"), man alone is capable of *giving* and *being* the fully valid answer of creation to God. Relatedness to God, which is essential to man, thus becomes a living dialogue in which man has the role of the answering partner. His whole existence is fulfilled in the fact that he answers as the one addressed by God. As viewed in the Old Testament, man is a being essentially related to the verbal movement of God; man's is a "response-giving" existence.

In passing, we should note, perhaps, that the biblical writings do not reflect upon or examine the response-giving character of human existence in the formal way we have presented it any more than the formulae which we have used here can be found in the language of Holy Scripture; nor should it be expected that all writing must formulate and literally state everything that is present by implication. Actually, more is contained in the implications of the Old Testament regarding response-giving existence than is explicitly stated.

In substance, the Old Testament is rich in references to man as the being *addressed* by God and called to *answer* Him. Even in biblical pre-history, precisely in its account of the Fall, this fact is given clear expression. Sinful man hides before the countenance of Yahweh (Genesis 3, 8). Here we may see, as in an antitype, how true human existence realizes what it is before the countenance of God and how sin casts man into unreal existence. But the account goes further and proceeds to mention that such an unreal existence of man is a silence before God, an attempt to disrupt the dialogue. For by His call, "Where are you?" (Genesis 3, 9), the Lord must force sinful man back to his response-giving character. Whereupon Adam confesses that he did hear God's voice in the garden, that he remained silent (Genesis 3, 10). From this encounter it is clear, on the positive side, that man remains true to his being only so long as he hears God's voice and responds to it, and, negatively, that the perversion of man's existence is a want of the proper answer.

To possess understanding of man as sinner is uncommonly informative for an understanding of his dialogical existence. That man is a sinner, what Galling called an "anthropological root-assertion of the Scriptures," despite the goodness of God's creation and the absence of all dualism in that creation, qualifies and perverts man's existence tragically. This perversion consists in the termination of obedience, in the egoism of wishing to be like God (Genesis 3, 5), in the disgraceful breaking of confidence that continually recurs throughout the history of Israel. Yet, even in his rebellion against God—man's attempt at monologue—the sinner cannot rid himself of his God because, first, he unfailingly knows of his sin and, secondly, he now experiences God's call in the form of divine anger. Even when hurling his "I shall not serve" in God's face, sinful man remains the response-giving being regardless of the falseness and blasphemy of his reponse and the offense he renders to his God. God, however, never exempts man from His covenant and dialogue. In the Old Testament view of man, then, it is forever true that man lives by being called.

The character of human existence as response-giving is confirmed in all those Old Testament passages where mention is made of the people's obligation to "hear" Yahweh. Clearly, the hearing which God demands implies alert readiness on the part of the people of Israel to comply with Yahweh's word and to live by His directives. In a word, the injunction to "hear" Yahweh implies man's obligation to reply to Him. An example of this is found in the opening words—"Hear, O Israel!"—of the great prayer which the pious Israelite was expected to pray twice daily (Deuteronomy 6, 4 ff.). Concerning the commands given to men by God, Deuteronomy goes on to say, "Take to heart those words which I enjoin in you today" (6, 6). The evident meaning here is that the Word of God should resound and find answer in the human heart. The very next verse of Deuteronomy voices a further command which shows Yahweh's concern that there be an answering echo of His Word in the life of man: "Drill them into your children. Speak of them at home and abroad, whether you are busy or at rest."

What we have been here observing from our scrutiny of certain Old Testament texts applies, of course, to all Israelites. It has special reference, however, in the case of the prophets, those "criers" of God who must proclaim the words spoken to themselves (Jeremia 18, 18; Osee 6, 5; Amos 3, 8) and, at the same time, serve as Yahweh's interpreter. For Yahweh has appointed the prophet to serve as His "mouthpiece" (Jeremia 15, 19). Indeed, much more decisive than the dialogical quality of the prophet's existence in relation to Yahweh is his relationship with the people to whom he must report God's word. In executing Yahweh's commission and announcing His word, the prophet "corresponds" to Yahweh's will and gives positive answer to Yahweh's special call. That the prophets recognize this obligation to make positive answer is clear from their accounts of their visions and of their callings (Isaia 6, 1–13; Jeremiah 1, 4–10; Amos 7, 15). The words of Isaias, "Here I am . . . send me" (6, 8), graphically illustrate this sense of obligation. If the prophet refuses or hesitates in giving his response, if he vacillates in his readiness to execute Yahweh's errand, then the Word of God works in him like a consuming fire: "I say to myself, I will not mention him, I will speak in his name no more. But then it becomes like fire burning in my heart, imprisoned in my bones; I grow weary holding it in, I cannot endure it" (Jeremia 20, 9).

By virtue, then, of the prophet's decision and of the response he has made to Yahweh, as well as by his determination to abide by his calling forever, God's word continues to live on among men. In Israel, the prophet came to be regarded as a "man of God" (1 Samuel, 2, 27; 9, 6; 3 Kings 17, 18; 4 Kings 4, 9) because his relationship with God was so profoundly personal as to transform his whole existence into an unremitting dialogue—a truth so vividly dramatized by the lives of Abraham (Genesis 20, 7), Moses, Samuel, and other prophets. Even though "man of God" is an expression of the most dedicated God-hearing and God-answering existence and may be ascribed to but a chosen few, still this exceptional phenomenon casts some light on the Old Testament understanding of human existence in general, and in a very decisive way when these same "men of God" urge the Israelites to deepen their relationship with God by seeking that same

personal, dialogical existence which the prophets themselves enjoyed (*cf.* Jeremia 31, 31 ff.; Ezechiel 36, 25 ff.;
Osee 2, 16–21; 14, 2 ff.).

In view of the central fact of God's revelation in words,
man is regarded as that being whose existence is realized
and fulfilled in his response to the divine *Thou;* man's
original posture, then, is dynamic and responsorial. From
this it follows absolutely that the theological understanding which is derived from Old Testament revelation gives
man a posture radically different from that to which he
is reduced when defined as a rational nature complete in
himself. Only when we regard man primarily as a person,
a subjective *I,* shall we begin to come to grips with the
full theological notion of man's nature. Only when that
personal *I* elevates itself to a *Thou* does man's nature
attain its full stature and concreteness. This *Thou,* in the
final analysis, can only be the absolute *Thou* of God, although the *thou* of other men is and must be recognized
as a true likeness to the *Thou* of God. (A fully detailed
Old Testament anthropology would set out here to develop
another element that is essential to man, namely, his
social nature.)

This is not to say that the Old Testament is to be in-
dicted for anything like extreme personalism or actualism
simply because the person is seen primarily as existing in
the act of the call and the response and because neither
continuity nor an essence of his own is formally ascribed
to man. But here it does become clear how open Holy
Scripture is to the personalistic demands of modern

anthropology and how fruitful it would prove to anthropological studies.

Furthermore, this fundamentally personal and act-oriented conception of man has significant implications for our understanding of human ethics and man's moral constitution. For the Old Testament was much less concerned with evaluating man's being than with determining what he should do. There is, to be sure, a certain ethical voluntarism in all this. Compared with the intellectualistic views of the Greeks, who regarded man's essence as primarily capable of recognizing what is true and inclined to the vision of truth in general, Hebrew thought viewed man as primarily a willing and acting being. "The center of gravity in man's essence lies in the power of his will."

Since the theological perspective of man's God-related, dialogical existence more or less predominates in Old Testament thinking about man, it is hardly surprising that the ontological question of man's nature is given little importance and is, in consequence, not developed formally. True, the Old Testament does attribute much less significance to the problem of man's essential make-up than is to the liking of a philosophical mind; at the same time it is not at all true that the Old Testament brings nothing to bear on this problem-area. Certain elements of an ontological view of man appear with regularity in the Old Testament theological, personal perspective on man, even though no specially independent significance is formally attached to them. Moreover, the elaboration of these elements can be very valuable here, because what Revelation says about man's ontological make-up is bound to be of deep interest and concern to us. Finally, the question of man's nature and ontological constitution is of far-reaching significance both because every part of man is involved in a redeeming intercourse with his God and because the concrete realization of his relationship with God depends, in turn, upon that natural constitution and essence.

D. "BODY" AND "SPIRIT"

Traditional theology regards the second account of creation as apparently making a definite statement concerning the nature and essential make-up of man and as seeming to speak of the two principles of matter and spirit (Genesis 2, 7). As a matter of fact, however, the distinction here between the "dust of the ground" and the "breath of life" signifies only that man is a living being which shares the transitoriness of all things earthly. To use this as the basis for a doctrine of dualism would be impossible, especially because the Old Testament nowhere has anything that corresponds to the notion of the body as the dwelling place (matter) of the soul. To be sure, Hebrew thought does differentiate by using the expressions "body" and "soul" (Isaia 10, 18), but it never proffers the two terms as signifying two opposing principles. For just as "soul" (*nefes*) can signify the whole human person (Genesis 2, 7; 12, 5; 46, 26; Exodus 1, 5; 12, 4; Leviticus 4, 2), so also can "body" (*basar*) stand for the whole man (Genesis 6, 12 f.; Psalms 16, 9). For this reason, the same actions and reactions are ascribed to the "body" as to the soul or the heart in their thoughts and feelings (Psalm 6, 3; Job 14, 22; Wisdom 16, 24). The original Hebraic thought, therefore, understood man as a living unity of which only two *aspects* are designated by the terms "body" and "soul" (or spirit). "Body" stresses the fact of man's infirmity and transitoriness (Psalm 78, 39; Jeremia 17, 5; Job 10, 4), while "soul," referring to the same whole human being, stresses his being alive. This unified concept of man prevailed until Hellenistic times when, under the influence of Greek philosophy, Hebrew thought was influenced to regard man as a composite of two principles (Wisdom 8, 19 f.; 9, 15).

The strong feeling in the Old Testament for the unity of man is of great consequence for his religious and moral life, reminding us once more how pertinent certain ontological considerations are to our personalistic and theological perspectives. For because of this unified conception of man, the Old Testament is able to give a very positive evaluation to man's corporal, material life and to preserve it from any suspicion of dualism. Consequently, the "body" cannot be regarded as the source of sin or the seat of evil, as is so often the case in dualistic systems. In turn, this allows for the view that human sin, which the Old Testament looks upon as a most serious and tragic reality, is not a natural phenomenon caused by the tension between body and soul, but is, rather, a personal engagement of the whole man against the absolute Person of God. Such a view corresponds with the predominant interpretation of sin in Israel, namely that sin is man's resistance to the will of God, disobedience and infidelity to the God of the Covenant.

Naturally, this unified vision of man helps also to explain the very strong Hebrew orientation to *earthly life* exclusively and the lack, from the very beginning, of any notion of the *soul's immortality.* The idea of the soul as an intransitory principle which lives on after corporeal death emerges for the first time in the Greek-influenced Wisdom literature (Wisdom 2, 22 f.; 3, 1–3; 4, 14; 15, 8; 16, 14). However, the lack, from the very beginning, of an expressed notion of immortality as well as of a clear belief in an afterlife, should not lead us to unjustifiable conclusions. For even if the Old Testament sets its sights almost exclusively upon earthly life, even if that spiritual asceticism or true renunciation of the goods of this life is unknown in the Old Testament, nevertheless in no sense is it possible to impute to the Hebrews any kind of materialistic philosophy of life. For the free, happy, and extended life which the Israelite looked for as the fruit of his God-fearing way is in no sense whatsoever a purely sensual, biological good, nor is it merely a healthy and long-lasting life upon earth. No, the kind of life which the Israelite looked for was something of deeper religious and spiritual content, such as the preservation of the people, the mighty establishment and continuation of the religion of the fathers, and, above all, the flourishing of the true adoration of God and participation in the cult of Yahweh. Therefore, what the biblical man seeks and understands as "life" is a vast and rich complex of values (without separation of the material from the spiritual) which are to be lived in the concrete. And this, of course, is again characteristic of the unified idea of man in Old Testament thought.

In view of the tensions contained in this unity of the Old Testament idea of man, it is understandable that time brought about a more distinct polarization of the individual elements of the notion and likewise their arrangement in vertical or hierarchic order. Thus it gradually came about that "life" was made synonymous with "happiness." This meant that an increasing spiritualization of the notion was already developing, the highpoint of which was to come later in the Wisdom literature: the idea of unlimited bliss in an eternal life (Wisdom 5, 15). But because, even in its spiritualized form, the material and biological background and earthliness of this notion could not simply be erased, Hebrew thought understandably tended to unite, even to identify, the earthly and corporeal with intransitory life beyond earthly existence. Because, too, of the propensity of Israelitic thought toward concrete unification of the corporeal with the spiritual, it was originally unable to express the idea of an intransitory life in the form of a belief in the immortality of the soul. The only possibility open to it was belief in a resurrection of the dead. The ascendency of this belief in the consciousness of Israel was made possible by a series of propelling forces. Among these was the thought that the God of Israel must possess power over life and death and that He can call the deceased back from the kingdom of the dead (1 Samuel 2, 6). The miraculous awakening of the dead recounted in the books of Kings gives abundant evidence to the ascendancy of this belief (1 Kings 17, 17–24; 2 Kings 4, 31–37; 13, 21). The generally acknowledged thought of retribution also made for progress in this direction. In this connection, witness the promise made in the book of Daniel that in the last days "many of those who sleep in the dust of the earth shall awake; some shall live forever, others shall be an everlasting horror and disgrace" (12, 2). Concerning the final destiny of the good and the wise, its language is still more graphic: "But the wise shall shine brightly like the splendor of the firmament, and those who lead the many to justice shall be like the stars forever" (12, 2).

Initially restricted to the Israelites, this thought occasionally appears organically bound up also with depictions of messianic times. The intense faith in the perfection of the final state to be brought about by the Messiah necessarily implied that those who had already died in a state of justification could not be excluded from His blessings. For the promise of a share in the messianic salvation was made unreservedly to all the just, so that limiting it to one generation (that living in the last days) could be regarded only as a contradiction.

Alongside this fundamental development of the collective resurrection of the just, we can, as of a certain period, detect a second development concerning resurrection as reward for merit and retribution for guilt in the life of the individual. Speaking on his own behalf and that of his brothers, the second Machabean brother said to his executioner on the very threshold of martyrdom: "Thou indeed, O most wicked man, destroyest us out of this present life, but the King of the world will raise us up who die for his laws, in the resurrection of eternal life" (2 Machabees 7, 9).

In the final analysis, therefore, the thought of the biblical man about his possession of intransitory life does not seem to be very far removed from the Christian conception of man's final destiny, even though there is missing the "middle" link between the idea of a frail earthly life and belief in eschatological resurrection—namely, the idea of the immortality of the soul. From the vantage point of our own fully developed Christian belief, this all seems to be a harmoniously organized unit, the yield of a continuous line of development. However, looked at in the light of Israel's spiritual history, it was, in reality, a very difficult process which led both the individual and the people as a whole through much obscurity, uncertainty, and despair. Nowhere is this shown more clearly than in the whole problem of human suffering in the thought of Israel. One must not suppose that because suffering has played so central a role in human living, any concept of man must be able both to comprehend fully and to integrate suffering within life's scope. This Israel was unable to do; yet, by no means did Israel, for that reason, remain fragile and isolated unto itself.

E. INCOMPLETENESS OF THE OLD TESTAMENT IDEA OF MAN; JOB'S SIGNIFICANCE

One of the truly great advantages of the Old Testament over the gnostic dualisms is that the Old Testament man experiences and endures suffering in its stark reality. Without divesting suffering of its reality, as Docetists have always been accustomed to do, and without romanticizing it as part of the great world process, as idealists are wont to do, the Old Testament squarely faces the phenomenon of human suffering. Old Testament man, at the same time, is aware of the basic cause of suffering and need in the world: he has always attributed it to original sin (Genesis 3, 16–19; Wisdom 2, 24). Because of his strong tendency to a hereditary view of human history, the Israelite views the entire panorama of human events from the standpoint of the Fall, seeing recorded history as the tidal wave of suffering and death which has encompassed every man (Wisdom 2, 24). Moreover, because of the Covenant and its sanctions, the Israelite necessarily understood the misery of his people as the primitive judgment of God for Adam's fall into infidelity (Leviticus 26; Deuteronomy 27–30). The thoughts of the solidarity of his family and people also led the Israelite to accept the fact that children were to suffer for the mistakes of their fathers (Genesis 12, 17; 20, 17; 1 Samuel

2, 34; 1 Kings 14, 1–18). Hard on the Israelite as was this explanation, it must have been vividly clarified after the national disaster of the Exile when such blasphemous and skeptical expressions were spoken in Israel as "The fathers ate unripe grapes, and the children's teeth are set on edge" (Jeremia 31, 29). This utterance, as one instance, expressed a widespread view that could no longer recognize the teaching of collective retribution which had prevailed in Israel until that time. For this reason, Jeremia and Ezechiel strove both to keep the understanding of God's retributive justice in the Covenant from becoming steadfastly fixed in its collective aspects and to awaken and keep alive in Israel's consciousness the truth of Yahweh's personal retribution to the individual. This started a movement which deepened and enriched the significance of the individual's entire life in the sight of God. Such an understanding of retribution regarding the individual could not give Israel any definitive solution to the enigma of suffering itself, as is evident from the very prominent attention given to this problem in one theme of the Wisdom literature. The author of Psalm 37 seems decidedly inclined in this direction when he sees the solution of suffering as lying in the truth that the good fortune of the evil-doer will vanish quickly and that the just man will not be unhappy for long (Psalms 37, 25). Well intentioned though it was, this religious optimism could only further the view which was later to gain currency in Israel: lasting and discernible fortune was proof of righteousness; serious and lasting misfortune was evidence of sin.

As may have been expected, Israel was never without spokesmen who prepared the way for a more profound theological disposal of the problem of suffering. The friends of Job, for example, are insistent in their belief that it is God who visits suffering upon man in order to teach and to purify (Job 5, 6 ff.; 8, 5 ff.; 11, 13–20; 33, 14–30). The idea is also heard that suffering implies an expression of love for man on the part of God and is intended for man's betterment (Psalms 32, 3 ff.; 94, 10 ff.; 119, 75 f.; Proverbs 20, 24–30; Wisdom 11). Even more profound is the view which makes the suffering of the just and of those specially chosen men of God an intrinsic part of the divine plan of salvation and which associates the service of God with a necessary share of suffering.

It must not be overlooked that these voices, pleading for a more profound theological interpretation of suffering, did not gain full currency in Israel. For one thing, the idea of retribution was extremely strong in the background. Furthermore, this theological development was hindered because of the utter lack of any idea of an afterlife. This is especially evident in that Old Testament document which deals with the problem of suffering in greatest detail and seeks a solution in theodicy—the book of Job which came into being between the fifth and third centuries before Christ.

It is purely an attempt at the dramatic to try to reconcile the sufferings of the just man with Old Testament revelation concerning God. The "hero" of this "drama" finds neither the theory of individual retribution nor the old theory of collective retribution to be of any avail here. The merely retributive justice of God is, for him, too small a yardstick for measuring God's greatness and man's yearning. And piety based upon the dogma of retribution in this life does not satisfy man's need of an answer to the mystery of blameless suffering. The answer is not to be found in a view of God and man that is limited to this world. Job already senses that the justice and wisdom of God unfold in a dimension other than that experienced by man in this world, that it can, in fact, be regarded as diametrically opposed to this transitory experience. This presentiment gives rise to Job's longing for a life from which death has been removed and for a definitive, redeeming judgment of pious men; it causes Job to utter these prophetic words: "But as for me, I know that my Vindicator lives" (Job 19, 25). Thus the drama of Job uncovers the instability of an anthropology which measures man and his intercourse with God only against the yardstick of an earthly retribution. The preacher also expresses the tragedy in his pessimistic utterances concerning the emptiness of earthly existence. It is here, at the end of the development of Old Testament revelation and belief, that the breakthrough is made to a higher conception of human life and its relationship to God, a conception in which the afterlife and redemption are sensed as essential phenomena of human existence and are even anticipated with hope.

Job himself does not yet possess this higher vision of redemption and man's destiny beyond the tomb. He is the symbol of the man for whom redemption and man's incorruptible bliss beyond the tomb are still unknown. Neither does he come in the end to share in any real solution to the problem of suffering. But the theophany of God (chapters 38–41) does finally permit Job to be silent and find peace, a sign of God's grace—bringing redemption in which alone there is positive meaning to the mystery of suffering and human existence.

The figure of Job may be taken as classic for the situation of the Old Testament man in general. Knowing himself to be addressed by God, the man stands with the knowledge that his answer to God, so indispensable for his life, risks being checked by his own sin and by suffering received from God; in a word, that his own inescapable earthliness stands between him and the response he must make to God. Accordingly, man's existence reveals a striking tension between devotion to God and the foreboding that all will end in frustration. Yet in this tension is the bud of hope that the distance between his answer to God and his very earthliness can be spanned by a bridge which God Himself will build.

Since this fulfillment has not yet been reached in biblical record, the Old Testament image of man is stamped with an inherent incompleteness which is made sharper by rigid attachment to the Law. It is as if the same veil lay over the countenance of this man that lay over that of Moses (2 Corinthians 3, 13), so that his face appears dull and lacking in natural beauty. It is the portrayal of man in the great Advent of salvation history, a man whose

undeveloped *I* awaits the divine *Thou* not yet revealed to
him in the flesh because God has not yet spoken that sav-
ing Word which He alone can utter.

Even shaded by Advent, this picture possesses classic,
timeless meaning and power. It announces the great truth
that, precisely in a world torn by sin and suffering, man
may rely on the revelation of a God who is near to man,
who will save man and overcome even an infinite distance
with His love, a God who, in opening up to man an
incorruptible life, will finally bring man to his real self.
E. Stauffer attempted to explain the spirit and countenance of the man of Israel found in one of the few artistic
representations that we possess from ancient Judaic times
—the representation of Esra by Dura-Europos. It shows a
man holding an open scroll of the Law in front of him
and looking seriously and severely off into the distance.
Behind the composure of this man lie the two spiritual
factors of the Law and hope; his face reflects them as
fidelity and longing. How different from the image of Paul
in one of the oldest paintings in the catacombs of
Domatilla!

This man has within him the profound fear of all ancient men;
he is as deeply conscious of the final needs and demons of
existence as any thinker or artist of Greece. But he is not only a
man who knows, not merely a man filled with the immemorial
tragedy of all things human. The majesty of the Lord has appeared to him high above the shadow of death.

2

The Revelation
of the New Testament:
New Creation in Christ

Not everything which the New Testament says about man is new in the strict sense. To the extent that it views man from the standpoint of creation, it is either moving in or simply presupposes Old Testament tradition (*cf.* Matthew 5, 17). Especially is this so of the Synoptic Gospels wherein Jesus appears as the herald of the Kingdom of God, as one come to reveal the Father. In the light of this revelation our understanding of man is likewise made clear: the characteristics that emerge are, to a great extent, those of the Old Testament man.

As man is revealed in the New Testament, he is a creature radically dependent upon the "Lord of heaven and earth" (Matthew 11, 25; Luke 10, 21). For all man's anxiety and striving, he is unable to "add to his stature a single cubit" (Matthew 6, 27). In all things he remains ever in need, ever subject to God's power and greatness; therefore he casts all his anxiety upon God (1 Peter 5, 7) and begs Him for the sustenance of his life (Matthew 6,

11). But God is the unbounded giver of life who can even raise up children to Abraham out of stones (Matthew 3, 9); in his care and providence man is ever protected (Luke 12, 22 ff.). Before this almighty and life-giving power of God, man experiences his own impotence which makes him incapable of the decisive work of his own redemption; man recognizes, too, that "with God all things are possible" (Mark 10, 27 with reference to Genesis 18, 14).

This profound feeling of dependence upon God, the creator and dispenser of life, is further developed in the notion that man is able to serve God through total dedication to His will. The New Testament also views man as a God-related being, whose essential relationship with God is in proportion to his service of the Creator. The demands of the divine will are to be satisfied unreservedly as is made particularly clear in the Sermon on the Mount (Matthew 5, 21–48). No rigid code for an elite few is herein established, but a universal rule of conduct for every man's service to his God.

Those New Testament passages which speak of harmonizing the human with the divine will bear witness to the spirit of unqualified dedication to God. That His will "be done on earth as it is in heaven" is a clear statement of the purpose and very substance of the disciple's life as well as his prayer. In making the absolute fulfillment of God's will his end in life, the disciple assumes the role of a servant who can serve but one Lord, who must do everything for his lord, and who throughout his service regards himself as one of the "unprofitable servants" (Luke 17, 10). On becoming a disciple, then, the life of man is wholly changed; "for if we live, we live to the Lord, or if we die, we die to the Lord" (Romans 14, 8).

Jesus has given us the noblest example of this high ideal of a life dedicated to God when he regards his own way through the world only in terms of fulfillment of the Father's will: "Did you not know that I must be about my Father's business? (Luke 2, 49). These words, spoken in the childhood of the God-man, are echoed in his closing days among men and reveal the consistency with which he lived the ideal of full dedication to the Father's will: "yet not as I will, but as thou willest."

The foregoing scriptural passages give some clue to the vibrancy of the New Testament idea that man discovers his real identity only in an encounter with the *Thou* of God. Those texts which speak of man's essential dependence upon God and of his obligation, as servant, to do God's will confirm the meaning of man's indissoluble *I-Thou* relationship with his Lord and God. "Belief and disbelief, love and hatred, . . . obedience and disobedience, virtue and sin—all of these take effect only in a personal relationship, achieving their colossal reality and efficacy only within the limits of the *I-Thou* relationship. Here also, as in the Old Testament, man's relations with God are understood to be strictly personal and dialogical, characteristics which bestow on human existence the notes of personal decision, actual self-realization before God and unique historical reality. The God of the New

Testament is the God who lays claim to man as His own and obliges him to holiness and perfection (Matthew 5, 48).

Inseparably tied to the concept of God placing obligations upon men is the "calling" aspect of the divine-human relationship. Men attain their personal fullness and happiness only when they "hear the word of God and keep it" (Luke 11, 28). Indeed, this Word of God, addressed to men and calling for response, was recognized as the true principle of life in the Synoptic Gospels before John came to define it as such: "Thou has the words of eternal life" (*cf.* John 6, 65–69). Furthermore, "it is written, not by bread alone does man live, but by every word that comes forth from the mouth of God" (Matthew 4, 4, with reference to Deuteronomy 8, 3).

At this point the New Testament continues the Old Testament way of thinking that there is life only where God speaks and man responds. And even at the high-point of New Testament revelation, the only begotten Son of God—the very definition of the life of the world (John 6, 48 ff.)—can be identified unconditionally as the Word of God (John 1, 1–14). But so determined is man's fate by his obligation to respond to God's call that it may be said that "of every idle word men speak, they shall give an account on the day of judgment" (Matthew 12, 36 f.).

That the New Testament is a continuation of the Old Testament heritage is further noted in its ontological view of man. The notions of "flesh" (Gr., *sarx*) "spirit" (*pneuma*), and "soul" (*psyche*), used to describe the physical essence of man are taken *in toto* from the Old Testament. Thus "flesh" signifies the living body (Luke 24, 39; Matthew 19, 5 f.; John 6, 51 f.), though at other times it refers to the whole man (Luke 3, 6; John 17, 2), especially in so far as he is a weak and transitory being (Matthew 16, 17; John 3, 6; 6, 63; Galatians 1, 16). This latter use of the term receives further development in Pauline soteriology and becomes "sinful flesh" (Romans 8, 3; 7, 24). Frequently the term "body" (*soma*) is used as a synonym for "flesh" (Mark 5, 29; Romans 1, 24; 1 Corinthians 6, 16), although *soma* has no Hebrew equivalent.

As vision widened, these three principal notions broadened. Nowhere is this more strikingly evident than in Paul's coming to regard the body as the shapely and visible manifestation or emanation of an inner personal reality. By and large, too, there is full agreement between the Old and New Testaments in the use of the term "soul" (*psyche*) as signifying the life principle of man (Matthew 2, 20; 6, 25; Luke 12, 22 f.; Romans 11, 3), yet it takes on wider significance in the New Testament where it may stand both for the essence of life as such and for the whole man (Matthew 12, 18; 26, 38; John 10, 24; Acts 2, 43; 1 Corinthians 15, 45). This broader understanding, finally, holds true also for the anthropological expression "spirit" (*pneuma*) because the New Testament also understands *pneuma* primarily as the spirit of life (Matthew 27, 50; James 2, 26; Apocalypse 11, 11), the inner principle of the human being. As in the Old Testament, therefore, *pneuma* can also signify the whole man and the person (Galatians 6, 18; Philippians 4, 23; Philemon 25, 2; 2 Timothy 4, 22). It is significant also that these three notions, used as they are in a purely anthropological way to describe the essential make-up of man, never imply a division of man into two (or three) essential parts, but express only the one concrete human essence from different points of view. This is so even when all three—body, soul, and spirit—appear juxtaposed in the very same text (1 Thessalonians 5, 23; *cf.* Hebrews 4, 12).

Yet, for all this, a glance at all the uses of these terms in the New Testament shows that the agreement here between the Old Testament and the New extends only up to a certain point. Paul, as we have already indicated, also uses "flesh" (*sarx*) as the very definition of man's sinful existence (Romans 6, 6; 7, 24; 8, 3; Galatians 5, 19–21, *et al*) much as he uses "psychical" (*psychikos*) to indicate not simply the ontological principle of life, but also the fact that man is bound to the earth and animality (1 Corinthians 2, 14; Jude 1, 19). In such instances, too, "physical" is placed in opposition to "spirit" (*pneuma*). Finally, Paul comes to use "spirit" to mean the divine power by which the Spirit of God moves and sanctifies the existence of baptized man (Romans 8, 2–10 f.; Galatians 5, 17).

In the face of the significant metamorphoses that developed in the meaning of these terms, the question now arises: What could have occasioned such a development? It came about simply as a result of a growing understanding of the redemptive revelation of Christ. The clearer the fact of Christ became in the mind of the New Testament man, the more his thinking had correspondingly to change. In the writings of Paul, therefore, these three ideas assumed an existential and soteriological quality and began to sketch man as already stamped by redemption through Jesus Christ.

B. THE RESHAPING POWER OF DIVINE LOVE

In recounting the earthly way of the salvation wrought by Jesus which terminated with Easter, neither the Old Testament nor the Synoptic Gospels could be filled with the reshaping power of God's love. Yet this power begins to take effect in the figure of Jesus in the Synoptic Gospels. Thus, in all those passages we have been citing to elucidate the agreement between the Old and the New Covenants with respect to the biblical conception of man, a second development is also indicated. Though it lies, to a great extent, only in the tone and atmosphere of the thinking about man, at the same time it necessarily leads to objective differences.

At first there is a slight difference to be noted in the purified idea of God contained in the teachings of Jesus. The Old Testament idea of God, built into the juridical thinking of the Covenant, was necessarily and preeminently characterized by the lordly, exalted, remote ways of the Retributor. In later Jewish history, these characteristics of a God remote from men developed even more as religious relations with God became more and more restricted to juridical and legal forms. Man's idea of God also tended to vanish with the diminishing of interior morality and religious life among the Jews, and human understanding of God tended to evanesce. In view of this, it is also understandable that speaking the name of God (Yahweh) was more and more avoided and replaced by *adonai,* the Lord. This fact cannot be regarded as proof of an increasingly purer understanding of God in the context of the general religious development in late Jewish history. On the contrary, it must be regarded as a paralyzing of religious strength.

On the other hand, the preaching of Jesus throughout the Synoptic Gospels has a loosening effect whereby the idea of God again takes on man-related and personal form. Full recognition and reverence before the greatness of the Creator is always present (Matthew 11, 25; Luke 10, 21), but His distance and remoteness are no longer exclusively stressed; rather they are noted as the background for the mystery of the goodness and loving care of this God for the things of man. In arriving at this dialectical unification of the "distant" and the "present" in God, the Synoptic Gospels have prepared the way for understanding the mystery of the Incarnation. "God in the highest" (Luke 2, 14) or God "the Most High" (Mark 5, 7) is at the same time the "Father in heaven" (Matthew 5, 16 and 45; 6, 1 and 9; 7, 21, *et al*), a name which may be generally considered as an essential characteristic of the New Testament idea of God.

It would certainly be a mistake to stress this difference between the two Covenants as if no bridge connects them at this point. For the fact is that the name "Father," in reference to God, is found also in the Old Testament, even though it is used only in connection with the Covenant and refers to God as Father of the people as a whole (Exodus 4, 22; Deuteronomy 14, 1; Isaias 63, 15 f.; 64, 3). In later Jewish history, the Rabbi Aqiba (d. 135 AD) was able to write with a certain pride of the unique relationship of Israel to Yahweh: "Beloved indeed are the Israelites, for they are called the sons of God. It is made known to them, as a special sign of God's love that they are to be called the sons of God." In the same way, Paul can also put into the mouth of Yahweh these words which are not to be found as such in the Old Testament, but which he gives as characterizing the Old Covenant relationship of men with God: "I will be a Father to you, and you shall be my sons and daughters" (2 Corinthians 6, 18).

Only in the New Testament, however, does God declare Himself to be a Father even in His relations with individual men; only in the New Testament does God allow men to address Him as Father; only here does the name of Father acquire its personal quality and inner warmth (Matthew 5, 45; 10, 29 f.; Mark 14, 36; Romans 8, 15; Galatians 4, 6). This deeply personal character of God-man relations frees the idea of God's proximity to man from the limitations of time and space and, at the same time, leads to understanding God as the "life-environment in whom we live, and move, and have our being" (Acts 17, 28). By the same token, divine worship is no longer restricted by law to fixed places and buildings; now "the true worshippers will worship the Father in Spirit and in truth" everywhere and at all times (John 4, 23).

By the name "Father," which signifies that man is primarily a child of God, the dialogical conception of man is raised to a new level and enriched with new substance. The cold relationship of a juridical partnership disappears and the seeming harshness in the thought of retribution before a demanding and jealous God is replaced by the warmth and gentleness of the new revelation of man's childlike trust in God. Divine-human relations rise to an "intimacy" which, in spite of many parallels, has no real analogies in either the Jewish or the non-Jewish world.

This child-father relationship of man to God has its most profound expression in the parable of the prodigal son, actually one of the truly high points of New Testament revelation in general (Luke 15, 11–32). It is, first of all, the parable of God's fatherly love which not merely embraces man as man, but embraces and draws to Himself man as sinner. The story of the prodigal son is also the teaching about a child's love for his father whose pardoning goodness is absolutely certain. Love, such as this, permits the prodigal son to say, "I will get up and go to my father" (Luke 15, 18). Beyond the immediate situation, these words are pregnant with symbolism. They mean that the divine *Thou*, toward which man is always moving, is love itself personified in the form of the

Father and that man's response-oriented existence is part of a dialogue of love.

The incomprehensible goodness of God the Father permits man to have that unlimited trust to which Christ, in the Synoptic Gospels, is always calling His disciples (Matthew 6, 19–34). The other side of the coin is the warning against a smallness of faith which cannot grasp the miracle of God's goodness and which reacts by locking oneself up in a stifling self-imprisonment (Matthew 6, 30; 8, 26; 14, 31; Luke 12, 28).

In all of this, the New Testament image of man acquires greater warmth and brightness. No longer do we view a man who grips the Law tenaciously and who looks into the distance in anxious expectation of the fulfillment of his incomplete life. Rather we look upon a man, enlightened by grace, who is already enjoying his fullness in Christ. This contrast is noted, too, in the new attitude toward the world that Jesus expressed and exemplified for men. Despite all the realism of His outlook on life's problems and hardships, the synoptic Christ never gives expression to anything even suggesting the tragic sense of life or the unsatisfied longing expressed in both Job and Ecclesiastes. On the contrary, even at that moment of Jesus' death on the cross when man would lose the sensible nearness of God on earth—even at that moment He exemplified for man the loving acceptance of His Father's will and absolute confidence in His love.

In this New Covenant attitude deeply rooted in a newly opened perspective upon eternity and everlasting life, man is no longer only travelling a laborious road toward discovering the full truth of eternal life; rather, through Christ, he is already in sure possession of this truth (Matthew 19, 16; 25, 46; Mark 10, 17). And that this everlasting life will also include the body is assured by promise of the resurrection (Matthew 22, 23–33; Luke 14, 14; etc.).

The light of these two truths dispels also the shadow of suffering in which man lives. The then prevailing Pharisaical teaching of the purely retributional character of suffering began to slip into the background (John 9, 3; Luke 16, 19–31), and human suffering, as a result of the sufferings of Jesus, may assume the sublime character of imitation of Christ. So it is that suffering now becomes a sign of the true disciple of the Lord (Matthew 10, 38 f.; Mark 8, 34 ff.; Luke 14, 27). So much emphasis is placed upon this mark of the true disciple that the New Testament hardly feels the need of a theodicy. On the judgment of Paul, who gives the deepest interpretation to the imitation of the Lord's passion, suffering is a grace in which he can even rejoice (Corinthians 1, 24). The deepest meaning of suffering stems from the consideration of future glory in the light of which the sufferings of the present lose their significance (Romans 8, 18).

A more detailed comparison of the New with the Old Testament in the use of the same terms regarding respective understanding of man will reveal a striking reshaping of this understanding of men whereby the New Testament will be seen as the fulfillment of what was promised in the Old—and this is the great determining principle required for tying the two Covenants together. With the advent of the God-man and the presence among men of "the goodness and kindness of God, our Savior" (Titus 3, 4), the human at last experiences that new dignity and brightness which the Old Covenant knew only as hope and longing.

The fullness of the New Testament understanding of man, however, has not yet been achieved in the Synoptic Gospels with which we have thus far been chiefly concerned. This is necessarily so because the synoptic Evangelists describe the life of Christ primarily as an earthly affair and avoid reflection over the timeless validity of its precise significance. This latter evaluation was possible only for one who could review the events from some distance and from a theological point of view. It remained for the Apostle Paul to effect this definitive and penetrating theological apprehension of the phenomenon of Christ and, at the same time, to put the finishing strokes on the biblical picture of man.

C. THE "OLD" AND THE "NEW" MAN

The penetration of the phenomenon of Christ into the life of New Testament man was possible only by a radical about-face and inner conversion. The experience of conversion in the case of Paul was a particularly intense one, for Paul had been a zealot for the Jewish Law and a persecutor of Christianity. The process of conversion shook Paul deeply because ever so vividly it divided time into present and past: by Paul's experience with Christianity, his natural, earthly existence has become a thing of the past; his true life has only now begun or, rather, is coming out of the future toward him, a life to be begun anew. In this way, Paul experiences himself as a man elevated out of the emptiness of past sin into the reality of present grace, the "new" man who emerges from the overcoming of the "old." And that "new" man never loses sight of this radical change within himself.

The positively uplifting terms in which Paul speaks of the new man fill the Christian with the inspiring image of man contained in revelation. To "put on the new man" to become re-created "in the spirit" of the mind and in the image of God "in justice and in truth" (Ephesians 4, 23–24). The Christian man will "strip off the old man . . . and put on the new, one that is being renewed unto perfect knowledge 'according to the image of his creator'" (Colossians 3, 9, 10). He will, in consequence, put on "a heart of mercy, kindness, humility, meekness, patience" (Colossians 3, 12). Above all else, however, it is "charity, which is the bond of perfection" (Colossians 3, 14), that distinguishes the new man. The "newness of life" (Romans 6, 4) consists in nothing less than partaking of God's own life and love, and in this way Christ Himself becomes our life (Colossians 3, 4). For the Christian man, therefore, "to live is Christ" (Philippians 1, 21). Sharing through faith in Christ's life enables all baptized persons to become "children of God through faith in Jesus Christ" (Galatians 3, 26), sons by adoption (Romans 8, 15;

Galatians 4, 5) who dwell as members of His most private household and family (Ephesians 2, 19).

But since the glorified Christ works this new creation of man through His *pneuma,* Paul can also speak of the new existence of man as a work of the Spirit and he can characterize the Christian life in general as the life of a "pneumatic being." In 1 Corinthians 6, 11, Paul tells us how Christ *and* His Spirit make the new man: "You have been washed, you have been sanctified, you have been justified in the name of Our Lord Jesus Christ, and in the spirit of our God." The *Pneuma* is *also* the Spirit which pours into the heart of the Christian that charity of God which distinguishes the Christian man (Romans 5, 5); it is the Spirit which gives man such "justice and peace and joy" (Romans 14, 17) as will pervade his entire interior life; it is the Spirit which, in the time of man's weakness, will plead on our behalf "with unutterable groanings" (Romans 8, 26).

In a special way, the new man becomes aware of the new freedom which the Spirit has bestowed upon him, for "where the Spirit of the Lord is, there is freedom" (2 Corinthians 3, 17). This freedom is something like the other side of the coin of love: where love is at work, freedom must be presupposed; where the highest love is realized, there, too, is the highest realization of freedom. Filled with the Spirit, man has, therefore, been in true liberty and "called to liberty" by Christ (Galatians 5, 13); he is now "freedman of the Lord" (1 Corinthians 7, 22). Let it be noted that the New Testament does not regard this quality of the new human existence as that freedom of the will which is presupposed for every moral action on the part of man; freedom of the will is regarded as self-evident and antecedent to this new freedom.

The freedom bestowed upon men by Christ means, in the first place, an inner ontological liberty from the shackles of unredeemed existence which thwarted not only the unbeliever and the sinner, but also the faithful Jew, bound as he was to the Law. Accordingly, in Paul the new consciousness of freedom frequently appears in connection with his rejection of the Jewish legalism which was supposed to protect man from sin (Galatians 3, 24), but which actually, because of its claim to absolute validity, had a dragging effect and even tended to incite to sin (Romans 7, 7–13). Liberation from such law makes the Christian uniquely mature, because, by becoming independent of human rules and standards of value, he may henceforward open himself completely to the divine will (Ephesians 6, 6).

A still heavier burden on unredeemed man is his enslavement by sin (Romans 7, 14), his subjection to the despotism of his own passions and wrongdoing (Romans 6, 17–19). To liberate the believer from sin is simultaneously to release him from the gloomy thraldom of death —the end of everything for the man of sin (Romans 6, 12).

Not only is redeemed man objectively and absolutely elevated to a state in which the enslaving force of sin and death is thoroughly broken, but also the new freedom that is his manifests itself subjectively and existentially in the grace-filled capacity for making responsible decisions in favor of God and His will (Philippians 2, 12). Clearly, man's new freedom, far from leading to licentiousness, implies rather a profound attachment to God—an attachment which is no longer experienced as burdensome compulsion since it is coupled with and held together by love.

Experiencing this positive freedom for loving devotion to God's will and, in consequence, man's own self-realization gives concrete understanding to redeemed man of the meaning of "the freedom of the glory of the sons of God" (Romans 8, 21). Only the man who gives himself into Christ's possession grows gradually into true human stature, into "perfect manhood, to the mature measure of the fullness of Christ" (Ephesians 4, 13).

Against the background of a conquered past, this experience of spiritual newness lends an uncommonly profound sense of adventure to the believer's existence. It is anything but the leisurely possession of secured property. For the borderline between the "old" and the "new" man, cutting squarely through his human existence, has been exposed by a genuine decision which he made and which he must keep, or, rather, continue to remake anew. The faith never lets man forget that he comes from the "old eon" and that he must keep pushing himself free from it if he is going to win the new territory and prevail in it.

The main reason for this is the fact that man's transition into the new life has not simply taken him, as a natural being, out of this world. Accordingly, freedom from the powers of darkness and godlessness is not a natural provision which makes the believer thereupon inaccessible to these powers. Paul's thinking here is absolutely realistic, recognizing the fact that the outward conditions of life and existence have not changed for the Christian. The Christian has indeed overcome these powers in principle and objectively he stands no longer under their compulsion; however, they can, in fact, still attack and wound him, since his redemption has not yet reached its completion and absolute power until the Parousia (1 Thessalonians 2, 19; 1 Corinthians 1, 8; Romans 12, 19; etc.).

Paul, therefore, thinks of the present existence of the Christian in tension-filled contrasts such as "old-new" (Romans 6, 6; Colossians 3, 10), "flesh-spirit" (1 Corinthians 2, 15; 1 Corinthians 3, 3), or "inner-outward man" (2 Corinthians 4, 16; Romans 7, 22). He is never referring here to simultaneous or juxtaposed essential parts in man, but to terms which touch upon the way and manner of his real historical situation. Hence there is always the real possibility of his earthly existence falling back into the life of the flesh (*sarx*), even though Paul, in the exuberance of his Christian existence, can only look upon that possibility as the most extreme contradiction to Christian existence.

The tension in which Paul sees redeemed man situated —and which John expresses by contrasting "being in the world" with "not being of the world" (John 17, 11; 17, 14–16)—is also expressed in the way he has his indicative statements concerning the being of the new man (2 Corinthians 5, 17; Romans 8, 9; Galatians 3, 27; etc.) followed by imperative demands whereby the Christian's new being is characterized as a task to be carried out. Thus he says of the redeemed man: "Rid yourselves of the leaven which remains over, so that you may be a new mixture, still uncontaminated as you are. Has not Christ been sacrificed for us, our paschal victim? (1 Corinthians 5, 7). Out of the "living in the spirit" comes the strict obligation also to "let the spirit be our rule of life" (Galatians 5, 25). The union of indicative and imperative in Pauline ethics is not rooted in an intellectual contradiction or in a lack of faith in the strength of man's new being. It is based rather upon his knowledge that for the completion of the act of redemption, just as for its continuance, human action is indispensable. Thus man, not by his own power, of course, but by virtue of grace, is a participant in the redemption which is progressing throughout his entire existence. The expression, "Become what you are!" makes a striking appeal to his person and calls him into the life of grace. But naturally it applies to him in such a way that he cannot become proud before God and rely upon his own contribution, because it is God who "accomplishes both the will to do it and the accomplishment of that will" (Philippians 2, 13).

In spite of the tensions to be experienced in true Christian living, nevertheless the burdens and pressures are not such that Christian life is necessarily without experiences of redemption. On the contrary, the Christian even

acquires the "taste" of the new existence, and especially
in the form of spiritual joy. In Paul's estimation, in fact,
joy is such an important characteristic of the new man
that he names it immediately after charity in his listing
of virtues (Galatians 5, 22 f.); elsewhere he sepaks of joy
as one of the basic effects of the *Pneuma* (1 Corinthians
13, 6; 2 Corinthians 13, 11; *cf.* also John 15, 10 f.; 1 Peter
1, 8). As New Testament exegesis has observed, it is
significant that this fruit of man's redemption is never
identified with the Greek notion of pleasure (*hedone*)
—pleasure restricted to the senses (Luke 8, 14; Titus 3, 3)
—but is expressed with the spiritualized notion of *chara*.
This very choice of words indicates that, for the man of
the New Testament, joy is a basic posture of the spirit or,
more specifically, "the joy of the Holy Spirit" (1 Thessalonians 1, 6); it comes to the baptized person not from
the world, but from God, and it takes hold of man in the
interior of his being. It wells up out of the consciousness
of possessing salvation in the present and out of the beati-
fying hope of its completion in the future (Romans 12,
12). Because this joy transcends all worldly fulfillment, it
can never be broken by earthly suffering (2 Corinthians
6, 10); rather, it covers the experiencing of earthly difficulty with beauty, so that the Apostle can exclaim, "I
cannot contain myself for happiness in the midst of all
those trials of mine" (2 Corinthians 7, 4). As a fruit of
the spirit intimately bound up with love, joy also reveals
its power to fortify and elevate the community of the
faithful to levels inaccessible to nature (Romans 16, 19;

Philippians 2, 2 and 17; 1 Thessalonians 2, 19; 3, 9).
Moreover, there are the Apostle's regular exhortations to
the faithful to learn to make room in their lives for joy
(1 Thessalonians 5, 16; 2 Corinthians 13, 11; Philippians
3, 1; 4, 4) and to rejoice with one another (Romans 12,
5). As in hardly any other quality in Christian life, it is
joy that, in contrast to all the paltriness and inadequacy
of natural life, reveals the abundance and brilliance of
redeemed existence; and it is in just such joy that the Christian appears as a real enigma to the world.

D. UNION WITH CHRIST

As we have often repeated, New Testament man experiences the newness of his existence primarily in connection with the person of Jesus Christ and union with
Him. Here the New Testament reaches the high-point of
Revelation about man when it pictures human existence
as an encounter and union with the God-man, Jesus
Christ. For Paul, even his conversion means an encounter
with Christ, and he speaks so simply of "him who from
my mother's womb set me apart and called me by his
grace" in telling of his decisive about-face in life (Galatians 1, 15). But this faith in man which corresponds to
that objective revelation, this faith by which man is justified is also "faith in Jesus Christ" (Romans 3, 22). In light
of this, the entire existence of the Christian can be interpreted as "Christ Jesus winning mastery over the person"
(Philippians 3, 12).

When Christian man is overpowered and incorporated by baptism into Christ's work of salvation, he thereby enters into a unity of destiny with Christ, nothing less than a dying and a resurrection with his Lord: "For if we have been united with him in the likeness of his death, we shall be so in the likeness of his resurrection also" (Romans 6, 5). For the fact is that all "who have been baptized into Christ, have put on Christ" (Galatians 3, 27). Furthermore, the union in death and resurrection between the Redeemer and the redeemed is no mere matter of time and place; indeed, it will continue throughout life, for "if we have died with Christ, we believe that we shall also live together with Christ" (Romans 6, 8).

"Being in Christ" may, in consequence, be accepted as defining full Christian existence. This very expression (*en Christo*) is found 164 times in Paul's writings. However, he does not use this expression only to convey the full sense of an ontological bond with Christ; sometimes he employs the expression as synonymous with the adjective "Christian" or as specifying a Christian way of acting. Still, in its fullest and most frequently used sense, "being in Christ" signifies Christ as "the Christian's sphere of life," the "Christian's basis for being and acting." Now this sphere is not a space-time phenomenon, an impersonal area of influence; it is, rather, the Christian's personal relationship to Christ as seen especially in the phrase "Christ in us," an inversion of *en Christo* (Romans 8, 10; 2 Corinthians 13, 3; Galatians 2, 20; Colossians 3, 11). Therefore the baptized person's union with Christ's destiny and life is, more than anything else, a personal bond with Christ in His "pneumatic" being, a union in spirit with the risen Christ, but, above all, a union with the crucified Lord (1 Corinthians 1, 17–23; 2, 2; Galatians 3, 1).

The life of the redeemed, believing man, then, is lived in personal intercourse with the Lord. In no way does this disturb or neutralize the original bond of man with God because this life with Christ is itself locked up and "hidden with Christ in God" (Colossians 3, 3). It is precisely here that the fundamental quality of the New Testament-Pauline conception of man's union with God finds its highest expression in describing this union as one lived through and beyond the God-man who is the appointed Mediator of the Father (1 Timothy 2, 5; Colossians 1, 26—2, 3; Hebrews 8). There is no danger here that man's relation with God is thereby interrupted or indirect because the mediation of the God-man is not a divisive middle ground between man and God. On the contrary, as the person in whom God experiences the fullest human revelation and through whom the Father becomes visible (John 14, 9), Christ leads every person subject to Him to that encounter with the Father and the triune God which will result in union.

To man's *likeness to God*, so essential in the divine-human relationship of the Old Testament, the New Testament adds a Christological stamp. In Christ, the God-man, the human likeness to God finds its purest and henceforward unsurpassable expression. Indeed, Christ is the "image of the invisible God" (Colossians 1, 15; 2 Corinthians 4, 4), "the brightness of his glory and the image of his substance" (Hebrews 1, 3). As "the image of the invisible God, the firstborn of every creature" in whom "were created all things" (Colossians 1, 15, 16), Christ establishes his own likeness to God as norm and example for all men. The elect especially are destined "to become conformed to the image of his Son, that he should be the firstborn among many brethren" (Romans 8, 29). Contrariwise to the man living under the Law, the faithful will all reflect "as in a mirror the glory of the Lord . . . being transformed into his very image from glory to glory, as through the Spirit of the Lord" (2 Corinthians 3, 18).

In the Christian, then, man's original likeness to God acquires a Christ-like stamp. Again, however, this likeness to Christ is not a static and fixed quality in man. Christ's image in man rather means a dramatic reformation, a continuing reshaping to the original image of Christ. In a word, Christian existence is not a state of repose in union with Christ, but a dynamic, ceaseless "straining forward" (Philippians 3, 13) toward "the prize of God's heavenly call" (Philippians 3, 12).

In substance, this dynamic advance toward the ever new and deeper union with the Lord is further characterized in the power of love for Christ (1 Corinthians 16, 22; Ephesians 6, 24; Philemon 5; John 8, 42; 16, 27) as well as for one's neighbor (Romans 13, 8; Galatians 5, 14; 2 Corinthians 8, 7; Ephesians 1, 15; Colossians 1, 4 and 8). Such love, however, is no emotional devotion to Christ that can be reduced to a certain psychical affection. Rather it is an identity with Christ's life and love which pervades the whole existence of man. Paul's words express this inimitably: "For I through the Law have died to the Law that I may live to God. With Christ I am nailed to the cross. It is now no longer I that live, but Christ lives in me. And the life that I now live in the flesh, I live in the faith of the Son of God, who loved me and gave himself up for me" (Galatians 2, 19 ff.).

In this inner union with Christ, man's existence in relationship to the Lord's person is not restricted to his own little self. Since Christ, as the new father of the race and second Adam (1 Corinthians 15, 45 and 47), lives among man as the head of a pneumatic body, the true man of Christ is placed into a community in which he will henceforward live as a member. "Being in Christ" thus becomes a "being together" with one's brethren. This gives the Christian some idea of the meaning of love for his neighbor and brother which is demanded so often throughout the New Testament. While it is an overflowing of true love for Christ (1 Corinthians 12, 26; Hebrews 10, 34; 1 Peter 3, 8; 5, 9), at the same time love of one's neighbor is the criterion by which is measured the genuineness of love for Christ (*cf.* 1 Corinthians 11, 17–34. The Christian's love for his neighbor is an unalterable condition of all increase in his love for Christ and of "fulfilling the law of Christ" (Galatians 6, 2). Therefore, the measure of one's love for Christ coincides with one's love for his neighbor; it, too, will go to the extent of the sacrifice of life for one's brother (Romans 16, 3 f.; 1 John 3, 16).

Thus we see that the fulfillment of the human person is not to be found in the restricted and isolated realm of the *I*, but can be acquired and maintained only by going out beyond one's own person to a *thou*. And it must be evident that where it is possible for man to enter into a living exchange with a divine person who meets man with genuine humanity, there is, in fact, a true completion of human existence. And this possibility has become an actuality in the Pauline depiction of the life of faith as existence ceasing in Christ and God, but an actuality which cannot attain to its full realization during earthly existence. It is, in fact, referred to a final revelation in the future and this constitutes the eschatological character of Christian existence.

E. OPENING THE FUTURE TO MAN

What is said of man in New Testament revelation, and especially in the highly concentrated theology of St. Paul, is a summit and a conclusion to which nothing in the past corresponds. Indeed, it is the outcome of the last, final events of salvation which were accomplished between the advent of the God-man into the world and His death and resurrection. As the result of these final events, the existence of the Christian is itself somewhat final and endowed with eschatological character. "The Christian's living by a faith which works in love," says Bultmann, "is an eschatological reality." This statement of Bultmann speaks of a purely present eschatology in which the salvation and fulfillment of Christian existence are viewed as an absolutely present here-and-now. Moreover, this here-and-now fulfillment is realized anew in every act of faith and, therefore, knows no higher fulfillment awaiting in the future. According to the message of the New Testament, however, the existence of the redeemed is something not yet present, something specifically "future," that is, stretching into a higher future and a fulfillment yet to come.

This future fulfillment of redeemed man's existence, moreover, corresponds to man's natural and realistic conception of human existence (in no way cancelled out in Christianity) which demands that man be viewed as always looking forward, ever expectant of what the future holds. It is even more dependent upon the nature of salvific goods bestowed upon the redeemed man. As with grace, with *pneuma,* and with union in Christ and likeness to Him, we are dealing here with realities which cannot be fully expressed in terms of earthly, temporal existence. Such realities, totally different, are absolutely perfect, absolutely beyond full representation in the limited, mutable, and imperfect world into which man has been placed as a natural being. In this world and in this point of time they are present not merely as promises or intentions, but as really functioning powers, though their present form is only germinal, even seminal. As a consequence, their manner of existence is like the seed (Matthew 13,

31 f.), or leaven (Matthew 13, 33), or the treasure hidden in a field (Matthew 13, 44), as realities "hidden with Christ in God" (Colossians 3, 3). And where they emerge out of this hiding, they must necessarily appear as not belonging (John 17, 14 f.), as strangers and exiles on earth (Hebrews 11, 13; 1 Peter 2, 11), and as out of place in the world.

For man, who is not able to grasp them in their full embodiment, this means that these realities have been given to him only as a "foretaste" and as a beginning (Romans 8, 23). And together with this goes the fact that he never possesses them and disposes of them in a permanent and secure way.

The tension between this for-the-moment, only incipient realization of salvation in one's own existence and its still remote completion confers upon Christian existence a quality of provisionality in two senses of the word. On the one hand, this life becomes conscious of its non-exclusiveness and preparatory character; on the other hand, it must look beyond itself and constantly overtake itself in its advancing toward the goal.

The first aspect of this provisionality is sometimes so strongly felt that Paul can speak of the earthly existence of the Christian as but a poor vision, a poor fragment which is destined to be done away with one day (1 Corinthians 13, 10). This is a vivid expression of existence in the faith which feels powerfully moved toward completion in clear vision (2 Corinthians 5, 7 f.), but which nevertheless remains bound to earthly incompleteness and can see its own reality "through a mirror in an obscure manner" (1 Corinthians 13, 12).

The other aspect of provisionality, whereby the Christian must ever go beyond himself, lends to Christian life the profound character of a *pilgrim existence.* Such pilgrim existence, as opposed to the inclinations of the earthly self to abide where it is, defies the world which knows nothing beyond itself. The incipient realization of salvation has such a strong tendency to completion that the redeemed man can only look upon the present world and his own existence as something to be transcended and to be cast aside. He can regard his mortal existence —and here again there is a similarity to the earthly life of the Lord—as a mere transition, as a constantly gradual departure from this form of world toward one that is higher. This is given graphic expression in those New Testament passages where the faithful Christians are represented as "pilgrims and strangers on earth" (Hebrews 11, 13; 1 Peter 2, 11) who have not found "a country of their own" (Hebrews 11, 14). These faithful have here "no permanent city, but . . . seek for the city that is to come" (Hebrews 13, 14). Their home, their "citizenship is in heaven" (Philippians 3, 20). In their yearning they look toward heaven as toward that out of which Christ will appear and in which the being of the Christian *en Christo* will at last be transformed into the full life *syn Christo* (Philippians 1, 23; Colossians 3, 4).

The pilgrim character of the Christian's earthly situation forms in him a decidedly practical attitude toward

the orders, goods, and concerns of this world, an attitude
which generally causes the Christian to observe a certain
distance between himself and these things. This is not
because he has simply discounted the world as nothing
at all and as worthless in the light of his higher objective.
By his sound belief in creation, the Christian has no part
in that faulty sense of values which would ignore or waste
the goods of God's creation. Nor does the Christian regard
redemption as an overcoming of creation in the Gnostic
sense, though he is ever aware of the tension between redemption and existence in his present world. Actually the
Christian has already overcome this present world's form
of existence; he does not regard it as enjoying first place
in created reality, and it has lost its absolute claim on
man.

The relationship of the Christian to the world can,
therefore, never be expressed simply, but only *dialectically*.
The Christian, on the one hand, displays a great independence from this world; this independence is not rooted in a
Stoic scorn for the world, but in his experience of the higher
reality of redemption. In early Christianity, this independence was sometimes known to have even taken on a certain disinterestedness toward the world and its values.
But apart from the fact that historical factors also entered
in here which had no lasting impact, this indifference
was only relative. Just as the Johannine Christ did not
ask the Father to take his disciples out of the world, but
to protect them from its evil (John 17, 15), so also did
the Christians of the Pauline communities realize that they
must not cut themselves off altogether from the world

(1 Corinthians 5, 10), but should take advantage of this opportunity (Galatians 6, 10) to shine forth as beacons to the world (Philippians 2, 15). A positive approach toward the world and their life in that world is, therefore, a mark of the Christian, as Paul himself acknowledges when he urges the members of the Church at Rome to "rejoice with those who rejoice, weep with those who weep" (Romans 12, 15). Accordingly, the redeemed man rejects all sombre and world-negating asceticism. The positive nature of Christian unworldliness is shown in another expression of St. Paul in which he advocates the free use of all the world's goods: "For all things are yours" (1 Corinthians 3, 22). Without nullifying the meaning of what he says, Paul does add immediately, "and you are Christ's (1 Corinthians 3, 23). Hence whether they "eat or drink or do anything else, do all for the glory of God" (1 Corinthians 10, 31). For the stress on these purely earthly things presupposes that Christ may also have a share in them all.

Although the Christian maintains a real orientation with the things of this world, yet that orientation is incorporated into a far greater, all-embracing movement in much the same way as the movement of the planet Earth is but part of the solar system. The absolute significance and validity of her orientation to the world have been seriously altered when seen in relation to the exalted Lord in heaven. In consequence, it may be said of this new Christian orientation: "for if we live, we live to the Lord, or if we die, we die to the Lord" (Romans 14, 8).

The distance from the world which the Christian de-

rives from his eschatological orientation is thus expressed
not in an ascetic devaluation and negation of created
things, but in a liberation from their claim to absolute
validity which was dissolved with redemption. It may
here be noted that the redemption, in opening up for man
the reality of divine fulfillment, elevated at the same time
even the created things of this world. How strongly this
inner freedom influences the Christian sense of life is seen
particularly in the fact that the instability and unrelia-
bility, necessarily proper to earthly things, no longer meet
the Christian head-on, no longer touch him to the quick
or wound him mortally. The Christian is able, therefore,
to live in want as well as in plenty. He has "been schooled
to every place and condition" (Philippians 4, 12) because
he is possessed of an inner freedom that ultimately covers
his relationship to everything.

The hardest test to confront the Christian in his freedom will come from the absolute losses and abandonment that are the way of the world, namely "tribulation,
or distress, or persecution, or hunger, or nakedness, or
danger, or the sword" (Romans 8, 35). Even in these
situations, his inner freedom gives him a security in which
he can say, "For I am sure that neither death, nor life,
nor angels or principalities, nor things present, nor things
to come, nor powers, nor height, nor depth, nor any other
creature will be able to separate us from the love of God,
which is in Christ Jesus Our Lord" (Romans 8, 38 f.).
The Christian's distance from the world culminates here
in an unparalleled superiority to the world. And it is with-

out parallel because it is not born of Stoic pride in virtue, nor finds its sustenance in earthly sources, but springs from the light and strength of the already powerfully advancing fulfillment.

How the Christian's eschatological "withdrawal from the world" and his *de facto* gravitation toward the world are related to one another, how remoteness and nearness are reconciled dialectically in his openness for the definitive completion to come is nowhere better shown than in the Apostle's inimitable words on the subject to the Corinthians. The Corinthians had obviously felt the tension of Christian existence "between two ages of time" and were not yet able to reconcile them. And thus Paul informs them: "The time is short; it remains as those who have wives be as if they had none; and those who weep, as though not weeping; and those who rejoice, as though not rejoicing; and those who buy, as though not possessing; and those who use this world, as though not using it, for this world as we see it is passing away" (1 Corinthians 7, 29 ff.). It is not the purpose of the Greek expression *hos me* ("as though . . . not") to inject a negative into the Christian's attitude toward the world. Rather it manages to raise this attitude to a higher plane and, in the light of this higher reality, to render this attitude greater instancy in man's life. But greater instancy is not enough, and something more substantial is called for here.

Be that as it may, this tensed posture of the Christian between the extremes of a salvation begun in this world and its fulfillment in the next can easily be construed as a sign of division or imbalance in Christian existence. It could well be that this tension might develop into a passion for incompleteness whereby the redeemed would never come to the joy of their existence. As a matter of fact, however, the tension in Christian existence does not take this turn, as is also attested by the Apostle when he tells us that we must be "always full of courage, knowing that while we are in the body we are exiled from the Lord, for we walk by faith and not by sight" (2 Corinthians 5, 6). From the realism of this statement, it is clear that the Christian does not exclude entirely from his thinking the possibility that the spread between the beginning and the completion of salvation cannot be spanned. Neither does he exclude, therefore, the danger of an even more tragic incompleteness in his essence than the man of the world experiences on a much lower level. But there is something which tends to close the gap between the two poles of tension, and that something is Christian hope, the real strength of man on his way. And it is this hope which fills in the emptiness between the beginning and the final realization of salvation, and which keeps the tension from breaking apart irreparably.

Hope is able to fulfill this function precisely because it is not merely a human presentiment and expectation which can be illusory and deceptive, for in this sense, even the pagans can have their "hopes," although (with respect to the true Christian virtue of hope) they "have no hope" (1 Thessalonians 4, 13). Christian hope, on the other hand, is an unfailing strength which "does not disappoint"

(Romans 5, 5). First of all, it is anchored in the already realized part of salvation; secondly, it is already stored and awaiting us in heaven (*cf.* Colossians 1, 5). Thus it rests upon foundations totally different from those on which Old Testament hope rested. Christian hope can, therefore, stand fast even where there is no more human ground for hoping, and the difference may be seen in the case of Abraham who believed, "hoping against hope" (Romans 4, 18). The Apostle regards Christian hope as absolutely essential for the life of the believer, for he equates Christian growth and progress with the strengthening of this virtue: "Now may the God of hope fill you with all joy and peace in believing, that you may abound in hope and in the power of the Holy Spirit" (Romans 15, 13). In the same measure that one's hope grows toward completion, the things of the future take on efficacy in the life of the Christian. In a framework of hope, they no longer stand motionless and ineffective in the inaccessible distance, but are already effective because they are coming.

The things of the last days, upon which the Christian's hope is set, do indeed lie hidden in the future. And yet, "brought down to earth" by hope, they still determine the existential present of man and make the completion of Christian existence visible in the planning stage, so to speak. This is especially true of the very decisive hope in resurrection from the dead.

It cannot be disputed that the deepest aspect of the incompleteness of human existence lies precisely in the fact of death. If it is ever possible to explain this phenomenon fully, surely the possibility of a fulfilled existence will also become graphically real. This actually occurs in the teaching of the resurrection of the dead which predicates man's overcoming of death by virtue of the resurrection of Christ. In a major departure from the Old Testament, this position forms in the New Testament a cornerstone of theological anthropology. It gives the redeemed man certainty that he is destined for an everlasting life. Because this life is endless, it cannot be thought of in terms of life as it is known in the world (*cf.* Matthew 22, 30). The form in which life is known in this world will rather be subjected to a thorough transformation (1 Corinthians 15, 51), the resultant form of which naturally cannot be depicted. Hence Paul's statements concerning the resurrected body (1 Corinthians 15, 42 ff.), for example, should not be taken all too literally as concrete attributes of the full life of the world to come. Their truth, however, is not therefore any less sure, for they speak of a possible conformation of man's life and body with the glorified body of Christ (Philippians 3, 21).

In this light it becomes clear that hope in the fulfillment of man is ultimately centered upon a participation in divine glory itself (Romans 5, 2; 8, 18; Ephesians 1, 18). Thus man is recognized as a being whose fulfillment and completion is reached not only by adding to his powers and perfections, but by virtue of the absolute otherness of the Divine Being.

Hope in this unique, infinite fulfillment transforms the

believer into a man with a tremendous future. On the basis of general anthropological knowledge today, it is an established fact that man requires the known possibility of a positive future if he is to exist as a human being. In the light of this fact, it is evident that the New Testament elevates man's existence in a way that has never been paralleled. Indeed, the Christian can only look upon the man who is without faith and forfeited to death as man without a future. But "to have a future" does not mean for him a merely formal openness to "God's being permanently ahead of him." It means, above all, existing in a realm which is filled with God's power and which leads him into God Himself.

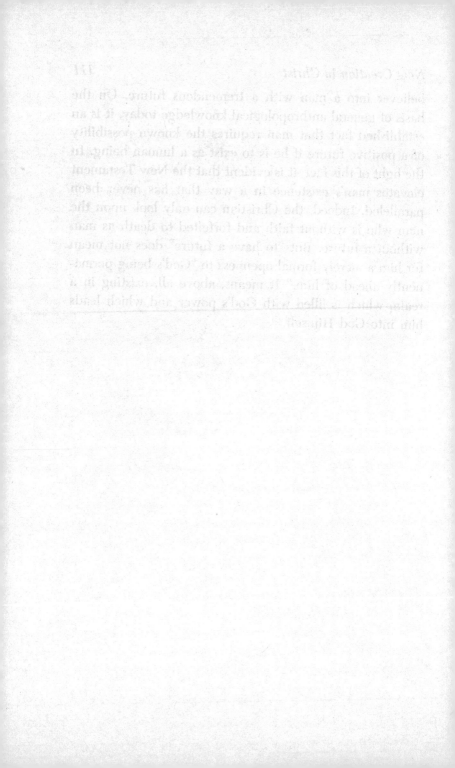

3

Confrontation of the Biblical Idea of Man with Modern Thought

THE TWO FOREGOING CHAPTERS traced the biblical image of man as it develops in the pages of Revelation. Such a presentation of revealed truth concerning man was certainly not offered to satisfy purely academic interest or even from the desire to know more about the subject. Rather, our study had the very precise and practical intention of bringing its conclusions into play on the current scene.

In the first place, therefore, we ought to ask the questions whether the biblical conception of man still has significance for the modern man who no longer recognizes Revelation as an absolute and binding norm in human affairs, and whether revelation can still exert any attraction for or influence upon the man who considers himself no longer bound by its authority. These are no rhetorical questions that may be dismissed with the observation, no matter how valid, that human nature always remains essentially the same and that the biblical understanding of man, in consequence, still has something to offer even to modern man. Even if one admits the essential immutability of human nature, however, it must not be forgotten that the historical situations in which man realizes his nature do change, that his relationship to himself and to the world changes, and that, in consequence, his inquiry into human nature and his own interests can also change. In this light we cannot regard it as self-evident that the biblical answer to the question of man is immediately understandable and acceptable to the modern world, even if the truth of that answer is not called into question. There is also the problem of whether that which is certain and enduringly true possesses a validity proper to these times, that is to say, whether it has genuine timeliness in the good sense of the term. Unless that practical criterion is met, truth, regardless of its timeless certitude, cannot really touch and take hold of the man of a given time and place. When that same man has removed himself far from the truth of revelation, it becomes still more urgent that the scriptural answer satisfy the practical norm of genuine timeliness.

If we now ask ourselves whether the biblical and Christian understanding of man has real relevance for our day, the temptation exists to give a quick and easy answer in the negative. Indeed, the facts initially seem to exclude any but a negative answer because the present position of Christianity in the world suggests that its ideal of man may have given way to new idols, that among those current idols it holds only the status of an interesting historical phenomenon and is fast approaching, for all practical purposes, the status of a museum piece. Travelling through Germany recently, the Russian poet, Yevtushenko, is reported by the press to have observed humorously that "Communism and humanism still rhyme admirably," a remark which won wide approval among the students. This isolated little episode throws light on only one of the idols which have been erected for the veneration of contemporary man and which may lead us too hastily to dismiss the practical significance of the biblical answer as wholly obsolete.

Obviously, if we are really to come to grips here with the whole problem of the modern relevance of the biblical understanding of man, we must first form a clear idea of exactly what modern man thinks about himself; the next step will be to determine where and why Christian thought has to take a stand in opposition to that thinking. In introducing our present study, we discussed in detail the cold facts which indicate that the traditional, unified conception of man has collapsed in our day. Now we shall attempt carefully to examine what men are left with after that collapse. The vastness of such an undertaking naturally precludes doing it in any detailed way, and we shall restrict ourselves to several representatives which will have to stand for the whole. Our procedure will be to take up those two most representative modern conceptions of man—materialism and existentialism—through which the main axis of modern thought runs and around which several secondary conceptions arrange themselves in their respective positions. Only then can we determine the significance of the Christian idea of man not only for non-Christians, but even for the Christian himself who, of course, lives in the same world and is surrounded by same attitudes as the non-Christian. Toward this end we must broaden our view and, by examining several representative proponents of modern positions, come to grips with the way contemporary man views himself.

A. FRAGMENTS OF THE IDEA OF MAN IN MODERN PHILOSOPHICAL THOUGHT

Varied as are contemporary non-Christian answers to the question of what is man, they nevertheless proceed, generally speaking, from this common premise: the man of modern times suffers from a disastrous division within himself. In the early part of the nineteenth century George Wilhelm Friedrich Hegel, (d. 1831), as a striking example, called attention to this situation and styled it the "self-alienation" of man. It is hardly surprising, then, that all modern thinkers should agree in their intention to liberate man from this alienation and to restore to him his intrinsic worth, his true and original existence—all this, to be sure, on a purely world-immanent basis.

Granted the similarity of their goals, the paths taken by different modern philosophers have been different. The political messianism of Karl Marx (d. 1883), who has become a model for a large segment of humanity in our day, regards man as basically a social and collective being which will be fully realized only in the perfect communistic society. Influenced by the negative philosophy of Ludwig Feuerbach (d. 1872) who complained that Christianity had brought man to a hybrid half-animal and half-angel state of existence, Marx came to a naturalistic and mechanistic view of history which also explained man essentially "from below," that is, as the product of external, economic circumstances. Man's spiritual make-up is, by this view, the result of the material and economic structures of the collectivity into which he was born and continues to live.

Friedrich Engels (d. 1895), co-founder with Marx of modern communism, describes man's coming into being even more precisely in an essay on the role of work in the humanization of the ape wherein he offers the explanation that primates were transformed into human beings through work. It then becomes Engel's conclusion that man, created by his work, is that being which looks exclusively to itself for its existence. For Marx, too, work becomes the essence, the self-subsisting essence of man. But since man became, by way of a partly necessary and partly self-imposed development, dependent upon the products of his labor, he found himself disastrously self-alienated. This self-alienation must be undone in a historical process; above all, man's subjection to man and nature must be removed. This Marx-Engels ideal will be realized only in the classless socialistic society wherein exploitation of labor becomes impossible, wherein man is liberated from subjection to his labor and to his fellows. Thereby is man's self-alienation overcome. Thereby, too, will man overcome religion and that belief in God which contributed so substantially to his plight.

Of man, as he will exist at the end of the development of communistic society, Marx speaks in the most exalted language. At that time man will experience the true resolution of the struggle between essence and existence, between freedom and necessity, between the individual and the species"; then will man finally take possession of human life and find the "totality" of existence. But it is here made immediately clear that this enhancement of life effects not the individual as such, but the life of the species, for the individual is a social being. How little the individual actually counts is shown in the Marxist answer to the enigma of death: death is casually disposed of with the assertion that the individual is only a being determined by his species and, as such, he is mortal. When we consider how every genuine form of humanism centered its whole attention upon the elevation of the human person, then we begin to see how profoundly weak and primitive is "socialistic humanism." In the Marxist contention that man is ultimately the product of economic conditions and is basically nothing more than a bundle of reflexes to material stimuli and interests is found still greater evidence of the weakness of the Marx-Engels proposal. Nor need we consider communistic practice in dealing with men in order to demonstrate the inner fragility of this "humanism." The contradictions in its theory are self-evident to the thinking man.

Nevertheless, hidden even in this titan of materialistic thought is the human longing for redemption from conditions recognized as not proper to man, from a state which has been somewhat correctly compared with the Judaeo-Christian hope in redemption and which has been called "a fragment of eschatology in disguise." This simple fact tells us that not even the perverted Marxist conception of man is entirely beyond the reach of the true doctrine of man's redemption. It is simultaneously clear that to those major questions to which the Marxist ideology offers opposing solutions—the question of the significance of matter for man, questions regarding man as a social being, or questions regarding the meaning of work —answers can be given from the Christian system which relate redemption to the whole man as a being which unites in himself material and spiritual principles, individual and social characteristics, immanent and transcendent reality.

That the Marxist theory of self-alienation and its proposals for overcoming it in the collective consciousness misses the reality of modern man is shown in the diametrically opposed attempt of modern existentialism to understand and explain human reality. Soren Kierkegaard (d. 1855), defining this alienation as essentially the ruptured relationship of man to himself, saw the cure in a reintegration of one's self. While, for Kierkegaard, this rehabilitation was to be accomplished on the foundation of a religious faith and hence "before God," such a possibility is excluded from the start in contemporary existentialist philosophies. If man is really to win back his true self, he must acknowledge the radical finiteness of his existence. However, this finiteness means not a firmly structured, fixed order, but precisely the opposite, namely the insecurity of his existence, his existing before undetermined possibilities, and his daily living with the threatening prospect of death. Thus all existentialist thought about man rests upon the common assumption that man is not a complete being subsisting in his own foundation, but exists only as a *constant becoming* reaching out beyond himself.

For Karl Jaspers, who is still credited with a most respected position among modern existentialist philosophers, this situation imposes upon man one single task: he must understand and accept himself as a radically open being which is moving constantly out beyond itself and beyond the world, but which can never reach its goal. Man, then, is a being constantly transcending himself without being able, however, really to lay hold of a truly transcendent or supernatural being. Thus Jaspers acknowledges the existence of a transcendent being, and he even refers to it as God. Jaspers further holds that man's essential frame of reference is this transcendent being, but, because it is truly transcendent, this being never becomes part of the world. The result is that man can never really know this being with any of his faculties. It is a being which acquires significance for man only as that which keeps pushing him back into his finiteness. While man cannot comprehend the transcendent intellectually, he is conscious of it only in enigmatic terms, in "cifers" which contain no objective truth that would ultimately enable man's constant movement to come to rest. The cifers are meaningful only in the fleeting character of a mere parable, which means that they reveal to man only the problematic character of his existence. Thus the meaning of his existence lies in the fact that he is constantly swinging to and fro between his own existence and the assumed transcendence or his presentiment of a higher being. In the practical order, this means that, in order to realize himself, man must sever himself, from all earthly certainty, all absolutes, and from all final positions and attitudes. He must refrain from reckoning with anything as final in this world and must always remain absolutely free and open to all possibilities. He will thus become a being who is dwindling away into limitlessness and whose only true definition is to be absolutely undetermined. In this sense, a certain boundlessness is ascribed to man. How poor a boundlessness must that be which fails to fulfill man, but which keep him in endless movement so that he will never find ultimate certainty anywhere!

Such an existence is destined not to fulfillment, but to foundering and failure. Jaspers therefore recognizes "foundering lying beneath all cifers of being." Precisely in this foundering does man make the jump across into his true existence, and this takes place especially in the crises of existence—suffering, struggle, guilt, and death. In the thinking of Jaspers, therefore, "the experience of crises and existing are one and the same." In crises existence is most intensely oriented to transcendence, but in such a way that transcendence is experienced only as a reference. In Jaspers' answer to the question of the self-realization of man, failure is the final word.

That man does not come to himself by this avenue, but rather slips away from himself, is the position of Martin Heidegger in his development of an almost totally opposing concept of how man comes to his own personal realization. Although the object of Heidegger's philosophy is not man, but being, his analyses of existence display a great proximity to anthropology, so that we cannot afford to overlook the implications of this field of investigation for an understanding of man. Heidegger sees man as coming into possession of himself through a descent into the deeper reasons of his existence. Man must, so to speak, bore into the deepest levels of human existence in order there to uncover the absolute center of human reality. What he will there encounter is neither positive nor elevating, for he will experience only how utterly and irredeemably marooned he is in the world, only how definitively he is destined to death. And death, as Heidegger explains it, means not a remote frontier for man, but a power determining and working itself into his entire life. The reality of death brings man "fully to his most personal capacity for being" and so becomes "man's most personal, abolute, and unsurpassable possibility" in which existence finds its fullness and man comes into possession of his true self. In this experience, which in man is translated into a profound feeling of fear, existence ends up by going beyond itself and so performs an act of transcendence. This does not constitute the acquisition of a really supernatural being; it means only stepping over and beyond one's self. If there is a purpose in this act of transcendence, it is not a higher, intrinsically fulfilled being, but only nothingness. Man's existence can, therefore, be defined as "imprisonment in nothingness"; man's attitude in the face of this situation is a "continuous commitment" to all possibilities of existence and the surrender of oneself to death. It is not Heidegger's intention to cultivate any kind of romanticism of death, nor does he advocate fatalism or nihilism in themselves. Rather, to Heidegger, it is precisely this nothingness in man which should bring him to higher activity and to his true personal being, but what constitutes this true personal being is not explained.

The resultant practical outcome of Heidegger's view of man is an attitude toward life that is not far from the deepest sort of pessimism and a nihilism which demands unusual heroism of him who would endure it. Since Heidegger's famous "about-face," however, when he reversed his point of departure (originally he proceeded from existence to being, whereas now he proceeds from being to existence), he has been attempting to explain man from the standpoint of being. Thus man's original determination to himself becomes an opening up of oneself before being and the expectation of a higher revelation. Speaking of salvation and of the sacred and standing in a quasi-religious expectation, Heidegger's thought has the romantic stamp of Holderlin (d. 1843). Decidedly, Heidegger has opened up a way to a more positive position; where it will lead him, however, is not at all clear.

In the face of these explanations of the essence of man, one may very well ask whether such a tragic existence can be meaningful at all for man, whether such existence does not appear totally empty. As a matter of fact, in a radicalism that is characteristic of the French spirit, Jean-Paul Sartre does actually take the step from the acknowledgement of the tragedy of existence to the definition of being itself as absurd. This radicalization of Heidegger's position appears at first in a closer bond between human existence and nothingness. Where for Heidegger, non-being was the abyss and bottom of existence, Sartre has it projecting directly into man's being. In his consciousness, or his "being for himself," man realizes that he exists in a rupture and that non-being is nesting in his subjective being, so that he both "becomes his own non-being" and carries non-being into the world ("being in itself"). This destruction which determines man means that man is not a complete reality, but only his own potentiality, only a projection of himself. Corresponding to this pure potentiality there is an absolute freedom which makes man independent of all orders, laws, and purposes, with the result that man stands totally upon himself and in his decisions is independent of all outside forces. Sartre himself acknowledges that a freedom for which there can be no foundation beneath man's existence is no blessing for man, but an ugly dowry which actually leaves him damned in his liberty. Carrying non-being within himself and existing as pure possibility in absolute freedom, this man is forced to seek the realization of his possibilities outside himself; he may be described, therefore, as a being which is "constantly outside himself." By reaching after things, man wants to attain to his being, but he succeeds only in bringing to them his own non-being; in this way man is only thrown back upon his own nothingness. Thus he is caught in a constant movement between non-being and being, without the capacity ever to close the gulf that opens up between the two. Theoretically, this gulf could be closed only by a being which is at once both subject and object, both for itself and in itself, which therefore is absolute— and such a being would have to be God. For Sartre, then, man strives for nothing less than to become God: "Basically, man is a yearning to become God."

Such an undertaking, however, is utterly contradictory and useless. First of all, for Sartre there can be no God in the horizon of absolute human freedom. In the second place, man's ruptured "being for himself" does not even possess the strength, in its negativity, to reach such an objective. Man, therefore, is a useless yearning, a being condemned to foundering and ruin, an absurd existence. That this understanding of man, left alone and consequently isolated in his own free decisions, is destructive of man's estimation of his neighbor is made extremely clear by Sartre in the *leitmotif* of one of his literary works: "Hell is other persons." Nonetheless, this basically meaningless existence is not to be given over to despair and nihilism because human behavior itself, in the eyes of Sartre, is sufficient to make this existence bearable. Certainly this is no convincing answer to the question of the meaning of existence, and this very incongruity is a proof enough that even the radical existentialist exists by virtue of principles other than those he admits or is even conscious of.

Compared with the intellectual intensity and radicality of the extreme positions to be found within existentialism and Marxism, other modern depictions of man seem mediocre and superficial. However, if the character of these teachings fail to impress, they nonetheless have impressive influences in the contemporary world. We have in mind particularly that human type so closely associated with Marxist collectivism (but not necessarily inspired or generated by Marxist principles), namely, the *mass-man* of modern civilization. A practical materialism lies at the root of mass-man's existence whereby he regards himself as, by nature, merely a member of one species among all living things, a tiny wheel in a gigantic process of life and work. From this view there results, negatively, the disappearance of the spiritual personality and, positively, man's assimilation into a monstrous, impersonal anonymous life oriented only to material goods. Such existence has been characterized with remarkable precision as a "consumer attitude." The loss of a being of his own makes of this man a plaything for all natural and collective impulses, an object easily dominated by any force which is quantitatively greater than he as an individual. Inevitably, then, mass-man is fertile soil for the rise of despots and tyrants in whose elevation the mass-soul sees a compensation for the loss of spiritual strength. The empty interior of such an existence can be sated just as readily by a fanatical storm of outward power as by despair and loss of meaning. This inclination of mass existence toward disintegration and destruction led Spengler and Klages to interpret the "massification" of man as a preparation for the downfall of culture.

In an effort to explain man, some have tried to brighten up the darker side of both the collectivistic and the existentialistic picture with a humanistic projection. Since its restoration in German idealism (both classical and romantic), humanism, in conceiving man again as a unit and by striving for self-fulfillment, has indisputably enriched the European spirit with untold natural values. But the more the idea of humanity was raised and universalized into an autonomous spiritual posture, the less it was able to embrace the whole reality of man. Thus in the nineteenth and twentieth centuries it continually lost more and more of its significance as an influence and power. Nevertheless, even today the attempt is often made to revive it and to re-erect it as a *weltanschauung* opposed to Christianity. Upheavals in the modern world and spiritual history, however, have uprooted its deep foundations and hollowed out its inner structure. Confirmation of this is noted when the advocates of this view of man tell us that man's being is determined by a "human motor-system," or "human impulse," which is essentially nothing more than need for prestige. The decisive driving power in human behavior is man's perfectly ingenuous vanity, his need of being able to behave selflessly and not selfishly, generously and not vindictively, fearlessly and not out of fear. A man who does not strive after all this loses his self-esteem. Thus it is a natural human need of prestige that drives man to keep himself humanly independent of all rational reflection or metaphysical obligation. It is clear that by removal of all metaphysical reality and of any pre-existing spiritual substance, the truly human is thereby clearly transformed into a construct of natural drives, so that man may be regarded as basically nothing but a self-contained reaction to the surrounding world. Hardly any deeper is that related "scientific" interpretation of man which sees him as only "a part of nature," which therefore sees human fulfillment as lying in compassion and in the increase of knowledge. Neither of these positions is anything but "a question of quality, a matter of gradual betterment of the educational experiment, so that here, too, man remains caught in his immanent material predispositions. Ultimately, of course, such positions lead to a sort of natural eudemonism as the most profound meaning of human existence.

A visible tendency is discernible in these positions to give a biological interpretation to human reality. Under the influence of Darwin, Nietzsche, Spengler, Klages and others, this tendency has remained more than constant in modern times. By virtue of a pragmatic openness to all human phenomena and its recognition of spiritual and religious reality as a directing principle in life, its recent expression has found no small echo in the world. Arnold Gehlen holds the position which takes as its point of departure the idea of man's uniqueness and special place in nature. We must, he tells us, erect an all-embracing system in which all human attributes can find their place and which will permit us to see man as a unified whole in himself. Gehlen's view is that man may be defined neither as a higher beast of Lessing's extreme biologism nor as a God-like being in the theological sense, but only in terms of his entire empirical reality—a reality which is ultimately biological. Accordingly, man is characterized as a being destined by reason and will—despite various physical inferiorities when compared with higher animals—to action and openness to the world. In the differentiation between deficient biological being and spiritual openness to the world lies the characteristic tension that makes man essentially an active being, a *homo faber*. The meaning of human existence lies in enduring it through work and action and in the living of culture as "second nature." Here the elements of existentialist philosophy, although losing their tragic pessimism, are tied in with the biological idea behind all this. As all-embracing as this projection is with respect to the empirical factuality of human life, as forcefully as it stresses the unique significance of man in all of nature, it nonetheless comes to an impasse for the reason that it attempts to explain man completely "from below." For in Gehlen's system, which sees religion and *weltanschauung* as regulatory factors in the realization of man as an active and cultural being, still man remains an "undetermined animal," which is to say, indeed, a higher animal.

B. BLURRING OF THE HUMAN IMAGE
IN THE MIRROR OF MODERN LITERATURE

The disunity in modern philosophical thought regarding man is reflected in the field of modern literature. However, what is given logical expression in philosophy is somewhat modified in the realm of "lived metaphysics." Such mirroring of philosophical thought in literary expression has, to be sure, this disadvantage, that the rigorous thinking which leads to philosophical definitions of man becomes flowingly confused in literary expressions. Counteracting this failure is the gain in the concreteness and the vividness of the picture. All of this contributes to instilling translations of modern anthropological currents into the life of even the average person. This kind of mirror brings modern man's understanding of himself much nearer to what is really there and gives it bodily shape.

The flowing of rigorous abstract contours through the literary depiction of man causes such elements of philosophical thought as collectivism, biologism, and humanistic immanentism to intermingle and blend beneath the surface. This is tantamount to such blurring of the human image that the impression of instability, mysteriousness, and homelessness in contemporary human existence is thereby deepened. It is easily understandable, then, why modern literature reflects so much existentialistic pessimism in its portrayal of man, a feature particularly observable today in what has come to be called "American realism."

The manner in which the representatives of this literary school of so-called "American realism" depict man in their works is a direct translation, with uninhibited openness to reality, of those things about which philosophical existentialism reflects with a certain painstaking subtlety. The contours of the human image become rough and blunted in the process of making such translations into flesh and blood. The striving for transcendence becomes a pointless stumbling within a brutal world which man encounters with pain and manly sadness. So we read in the foreword of Thomas Wolfe's novel, *You Can't Go Home Again,* as characteristic of his hero:

There came to him an image of man's whole life upon the earth. It seemed to him that all man's life was like a tiny spurt of flame that blazed out briefly in an illimitable and terrifying darkness, and that all man's grandeur, tragic dignity, his heroic glory, came from the brevity and smallness of this flame. He knew his life was little and would be extinguished, and that only darkness was immense and everlasting. And he knew that he would die with defiance on his lips, and that the shout of his denial would ring with the last pulsing of his heart into the maw of all-engulfing night.

There is also a definite deeper meaning in the fact that this novel begins with a chapter entitled "The Drunken Beggar on Horseback" which suits perfectly a man who has been torn from his center, who has lost his inner grip on reality, and who is now driven to and fro by impersonal forces. Of these, physical love invariably plays a leading role, and the impression is strong that human relations are restricted to the physical level. This school also has a great preference for stranded destinies, as we so often find in Steinbeck's *The Pastures of Heaven* or in O'Neill's plays, about which it has been said that they all depict "man's marathon into despair."

Ernest Hemingway's characters too are all spiritually homeless beings who put up a fight against brutal reality and, in doing so, become ugly and primitive themselves. Harry Fisher Morgan in *To Have and Have Not* comes immediately to mind, a man who would like to remain upright and good, but becomes a merciless murderer in spite of himself. Such men have lost their humanity. When asked by a critic why he represented man as so primitive and brutelike, Hemingway is supposed to have said, "I only hold a mirror up to men. It is not my fault if an ape peers out of it." It has been observed that Hemingway never really speaks about *man*, but only about *a man*, and specifically a "manly" man. This Hemingway character is really not heroic at all, but a fighter who lacks all sentiment and is always on the defensive in an opposing world —a world which is not really distinct or clear. It is not explicitly asserted that a new human dimension could ever emerge from this struggle, although this is ever so faintly heard here and there in the writer's works taken as a whole. As an example here, we can cite *The Old Man and the Sea.*

More evidence of such pessimistic tendencies in the modern American novel could be built up at will. We could go on to consider Dos Passos or Faulkner whose works always show man as impotent either in his struggle with the forces of the universe or in his debasement as a consequence of the daily existence to which he is condemned.

Where the American novel can be considered as outstanding for its realism, much of European writing is superior by virtue of its intellectual depth and subtlety. In this reference we may consider the literary work of Thomas Mann as exemplary. The man he portrays differs outwardly from the existential coarseness of American realism because he displays an inclination toward the personal and the human and toward the proper interpretation of these at any cost. This man may be regarded as more human even for his very doubt about coarser values. In Mann's *Magic Mountain* (1925), the humanist, Sttembrini, is "forever blowing the horn of reason" which is "narrow-mindedness and mere moralism." Opposed to Sttembrini's estimate is the "poetic dream about man" which the hero of the book, Hans Castorp, experiences and expresses: "Man is the lord of counter-positions, they can be only through him, and he is more aristocratic than they. More so than death, too aristocratic for death—that is the freedom of his mind. More aristocratic than life, too aristocratic for life, and that is the piety of his heart." Then follows the maxim: "I will be good. I will let death have no mastery over my thoughts. For therein lies goodness and love of mankind, and in nothing else." However, this positive statement of Mann's hero is subsequently disavowed in the facts of the story when Castorp dies a meaningless death on a battlefield of the great war. As is generally true in Mann's early works, we note here a pessimistic irony conveying undertones of Schopenhauer and Nietzsche.

The brooding darkness of this tragic twilight seems to brighten up only in the Goethe-type novel, *Lotte in Weimar* (1939), wherein we are given a very much alive and full person in Lotte herself. But the main character is the brilliant poet in whom the author sees something unfathomably demoniacal at work—a reference to the irrational and the enigmatic in human nature. Mann's *Doctor Faustus* (1948) contains his most forceful expression of this notion. *Doctor Faustus* not only details the great German tragedy, but it seeks to expose the abnormality, the equivocality, the frustration of existence through the person and fate of Adrian Leverkuhn. The modern Doctor Faustus, exemplar of man in a crumbling world, is a mad fanatic who has foresworn all humanism and who reckons with the demonic as the fundamental reality in the world of men. Through music, which he regards as the revelational force of the irrational depths, he seeks access to the demonic kingdom to which he must subscribe formally in the end. His way through the world of appearances, dissolution, and spiritual emptiness, where it is already evident that all culture will soon be turned into barbarism, ends in spiritual collapse—a sign of the victorious power of the demonic element in man. Naturally one could assume that the very conjuration of the devil implies the recognition of a good and divine principle which gives structure to this picture of man and the world. And this structure might, in spite of the apparent chaos behind it all, permit us at least to suspect some order in it. However, this devil has no opposite; rather, he is the expression of the absolute hegemony of the tragic and the destructive in man's being. So that Grenzmann's very penetrating and lucid analysis of *Doctor Faustus* is decidedly to the point: "The work is nothing more than the German expression of that existentialistic despair which is so native to French epic and drama." The man pictured as delivered up to the demoniacal is the opposite of the man in grace. He is the incarnation of the non-being within himself which becomes an irresistible power.

To our assertion that Thomas Mann's final word concerning man is basically pessimistic, objection may be made that Mann, in his *Felix Krull*, seems in the end to have created a cheerfully buoyant and conciliatory character in contrast to the somber depiction of man in *Doctor Faustus;* or it may be further urged that Mann has successfully justified the tragic by reconciling it, through its opposite, into a higher unity. Such interpretation is at least difficult in understanding the vagrant imposter, Felix

Krull, who assimilates the sham and illusion that this world really is through disguise, deception, and pretense. Rather, from *Felix Krull* emerges the impression that human existence is ultimately protean and pervaded with idle phantasms, that it knows no real permanence or subsistence, and that it is occupied entirely with appearances —a strange turn for the "nothingness" thesis of man to take.

In Thomas Mann, this tragic note is repeatedly broken by irony and is elevated by the superb use of artistic and esthetic technique into a fascinating superabundance of sheer light. In Franz Kafka, on the other hand, the same tragedy is depicted with intentional economy of expression and, at the same time, with clocklike precision. As man appears in the unbelievable realism of Kafka's dream world, he is a being helplessly driving and being driven in a meaningless reality. He lives in the depressing certainty that the meaning of his existence is lost, and in the ominous fear that his end will be his total annihilation. Accordingly, Kafka's main novels, *The Trial* (1925), *The Castle* (1926), *America* (1927), are so constructed that in the end the hero perishes in disgrace. In *The Trial* the hero is killed "like a dog" by the executioners of an anonymous court; in *America* he is "more pushed lightly aside than thrown down"; in *The Castle* he dies of exhaustion before the arrival of the long-awaited message. The existence of Kafka's man always comes to the point of despair against a background full of incomprehensibility, disruption, discontinuity, and destruction. Continually torn between irreconcilables, man lives a nightmare, one ugly symbol of which is the figure of Gregory Samsa who is transformed into a vermine.

In the beginning of the short story, *A Country Doctor,* man's "great difficulty" is vividly exemplified. A doctor is called to visit a sick man. Yet he knows that he should remain at home in order to protect his housemaid from the violent intentions of a stranger. In the end, however, the doctor feels compelled to go to the sick man whom he finds, on first inspection, to be in perfect health. A more careful examination reveals, however, that the man has an incurable wound on his body. Convinced that no cure is possible, the doctor sets out for home. On the way he becomes fully disheartened because of his tired horse and the endless wastes of snow. "I'll never get home this way," he thinks, and by this expression of thought Kafka shows the uselessness of all human efforts to gain a sure footing in this world. "Deceived! Deceived!" at the end of the story expresses the fact of a deceptive world as well as man's enigmatic and futile existence.

Kafka's interpretation of man through his novels is only one voice in the chorus of those moderns who despair of man and who surrender his essence to non-being. One might even say that, from the standpoint of real human experience, Franz Kafka reaches the nadir of modern man's experience of himself. We note also, however, the remarkable dialectic that underlies the thought here. For it is already possible at this point to detect the change that shows some promise of hope. This brings us to the fundamental question of whether there are not, indeed, some contact-points in Kafka and others for a confrontation between the biblical understanding of man and modern anthropological thought, contact-points which just possibly may serve as a definite preparatory basis for understanding the Christian message and keeping that message from falling into an absolute vacuum.

C. THE PROBLEM OF CONTACT-POINTS

The yield of our cursory survey of man's self-depiction in modern times is hardly encouraging for the Christian observer. In witnessing this dance of the will-of-the-wisp calling one into the abyss, we can only be more urgent in our original inquiry into whether the Christian understanding of man can still clarify, or enlighten, or have any effect whatsoever in confronting a conception of man that has been distorted even to the point of unrecognizability. An answer in the negative almost forces itself upon us, yet we must not allow ourselves to be overly influenced by the negative first impression. The fact of the matter is that here and there in this dark landscape of human reality there are helpful beams of light, and they appear to indicate that, even for this consciously faithless thinking about man, the low point in despair itself proves to be the initial stage of a turning—a turning at least to reflection about a positive purpose. Kafka's own diary, in which he refers to his novels in unveiled terms, would seem to justify this observation. Thus the quotation in Brod's biography of

Kafka: "Man cannot live without constant trust in something that is indestructible in itself." The following entry in Kafka's diary points in the same direction: "I can still find temporary satisfaction in writings like *The Country Doctor* . . . but I can find true happiness if I can sublimate the world into the Pure, the True, the Unchangeable." Here we find a budding hope for liberation and redemption from the doom of existence. And at one point in the diary, this hope is even tied to the person of the Redeemer, Christ: "Christ! What a light-filled abyss! One must close one's eyes, so as to resist jumping off into such brightness." Even the characters of Kafka's novels, so enmeshed in the entanglements of existence and so conscious of the futility and fearfulness of life, bear witness to the existence of someone who could redeem them and make them whole, even though such witnessing is indistinct in the haze of an estranged world. The land-surveyor (in Kafka's *The Castle*) who seeks in vain to gain access to the castle testifies, in spite of his failure, that there is a transcendent reality for man. And the surveyor's final words, "He who seeks, will not find; he who does not seek, will be found," intimate that it is not man's fault that he is not found.

This very notion of fault, so strong throughout Kafka, opens up a new vision of positive realities. It pervades especially the nightmarish scenery of *The Trial*. Even though the man who is accused by an invisible authority cannot grasp the reason for its verdict of guilty, and even though he revolts against it from time to time, still the

confession is present in the depths of the accused's consciousness that in some mysterious sense he has become
guilty. At the same time, the accused man also recognizes
the existence of a judging authority. The entire negative
quality in man's present condition thus becomes understandable as a perversion that should not have been, and,
where perversion is seen in that light, the sense of a valid
order and the feeling for the possibility of its restoration
have already begun to take form. To be sure, man in this
state remains a being fatally driven by forces he does not
know. But in being driven, man comes to long for the
"totally other," for the purposefulness and meaningfulness
of his tragic movement: "The chase goes through me and
tears me apart—but help is waiting somewhere, and the
drivers are steering me there." Thus Kafka's tragic and
meaningless picture of man can be understood as a "negative theology" which points the way beyond negation to
a transcendent reality as yet unknown and incomprehensible. The meaninglessness here actually evokes the new
meaning, even though this meaning seems unattainable
for the present. The Christian answer of a fulfillment that
has already taken place can no longer be wholly misunderstood by the man who has experienced the vacuum.

A quite different situation arises when, as in Thomas
Mann, consciousness of fault and perversion is lacking.
Where disorder is no longer experienced as a fall, but as
something essential and belonging to being, the thought
of a new ascent cannot even be conceived. Where there
is no consciousness of sin, an understanding of grace will
necessarily be lacking. This is actually the case with

Thomas Mann, at least in his depiction of man and the world in *Doctor Faustus*. If man and the world belong by their very nature to the irrational and the chaotic, then the end can only be total dissolution in chaos. This, at least, is the logical consequence of the basic position man once elected for himself. But there is a question as to whether such a spiritual structure is enough for man and whether he will not, in a deeper level of his being, deny again the absolute negation. Indeed, this negation of total negation is evidently a work wherever, within the framework of annihilating forces and despair, a glimmer of hope begins to shine. This occurs even in *Doctor Faustus* where reference is made to a "light in the night." Have we not here an expression of "hoping against hope"? Is it not as much as saying "that an unbelieved, unknown, unworshipped God comes with mercy and redemption to the aid of this miserable world that is so involved in itself?" In a pessimistic conception of man that claims to be purely immanentistic, such a burgeoning of meaning and hope is actually a self-contradiction; and yet, from the standpoint of the idea of Revelation, this contradiction is perfectly logical. It proves that, contrary to the conscious intentions of the pessimist, man cannot live in the prison of a nihilistic immanentism, that he is oriented to a purpose which is greater than himself and which is so powerfully real that it will prevail even in the most radical denial of its existence. Where this occurs, there is an opening through which the word of the Christian can find entrance to the spirit of modern man.

Even in the transitoriness and despair of the human

situation as it is depicted by American realism, even in
the futile passion for mortal life, we occasionally hear
things which remind man in his meaninglessness of something greater and indestructible. In Hemingway's *For
Whom the Bell Tolls*, it is the experience of human love
in the midst of a deserted, destruction-scarred landscape
that opens up a vision of something worthwhile wrenched
from destruction, something permanent in man. And this
is all the more remarkable in the light of the wild propor-
tions and pagan worldliness of the love itself. At the end
of the novel, Robert Jordan, freedom fighter and the very
essence of a purely mortal man, admits that what he once
said in the face of death is true, that love has the power to
conquer death: "It does no good to think about Maria.
Try to believe what you told her. That is the best. And
who says it is not true? Not you." It is not without cause,
therefore, that Jordan turns to the question of God in his
final thoughts: "Who do you suppose has it easier? One
with religion or just taking it straight?" Even if the answer
says only, "It comforts them very much, but we know
there is nothing to fear," still that answer allows us that
immanence has broken through here and that the possibility of transcendence is within man's ken, even though
not comprehended. And the *credo* at the end of Thomas
Wolfe's *You Can't Go Home Again* makes our point still
clearer: "To lose the earth you know, for greater knowing;
to lose the life you have, for greater life; to leave the
friends you loved, for greater loving; to find a land more
kind than home, more large than earth . . ."

And so it appears that modern thinking about man, as reflected in modern fiction, is open at various points, in spite of its declared pessimistic purposes, to transcendence and consequently to the Christian answer to the puzzle of man. This opening and the transcending to which it points appear in various forms: in recognizing a higher salvation even in the very denial of salvation as man's goal (Kafka); in the unconscious denial of nihilism through a hope against all hope (Mann); in the experience of the transparency of earthly things through which something entirely different is seen (Hemingway, Wolfe).

This identical observation can be made regarding certain philosophical projections of man even, in fact, in the consciously atheistic view of man in Jean-Paul Sartre. Sartre seems to be the most radical in isolating man in his nothingness and in placing him under the curse of an existence that is impossible of fulfillment. Yet this very destiny of unfulfillment points formally to something absolute, for man is the unattainable desire to become God. Sartre's thought is remarkable not only for its use of the religious notion, "God," but also for his expressions of such other notions of the same origin as hell, the devil, original sin. Although these ideas, as used by Sartre, are divested of their original content, they nevertheless indicate that Sartre's thought cannot divest itself of opposition to Christian thought. Indeed, opposition to the Christian God is so basic and essential to his thought that his system would collapse without it. This implies that Sartre's radically atheistic man, in order to maintain the reality of his titanic decision against God, must presuppose the existence of God behind it all. He who can exist only on a protest against God, who can realize himself only by denying God is acknowledging, in spite of himself, that God is no invention of human fancy, but a reality. Sartre's atheistic humanism projects an image of man that is definitely a perversion of the Christian man; still, even in the perversion and precisely because it is so radical, the contours of the original image remain visible. Here, too, we notice that, if we consider the situation objectively, it is not impossible to link up even Sartre's thought with the Christian understanding of man.

In another direction, as we have already indicated, an openness for a positive transcendent reality can be found in Heidegger's thought. As a result of his "about-face" which we described earlier, man, according to Heidegger, is shifted over into the proximity of being which is a "dimension of salvation." This has important consequences because "the truth of being permits one to consider the essence of the holy," and "the essence of the holy permits one to consider the essence of the divinity." To be sure, our age and world are still determined by the absence and "lack of God," but when there is a clear vision of being, it is then possible for "the day of the holy to dawn" and an "appearance of God and of the gods can be seen anew." Then will man find his way back from the homeless condition in which he finds himself.

Because of the indecisiveness and ambivalence of these statements, the religious motif is surely not identical with

Christian belief; but neither does it stand in inflexible opposition to Christian belief. Where the question of salvation is posed so openly, the Christian answer to the question can no longer be entirely ignored; and even if the Christian reply is not received and accepted as satisfying, it still can be and must be considered as a possibility.

Because Jaspers feels so strongly about the need all men have for communication, consideration of the Christian answer to the question of man is taken for granted. For this reason, in Jaspers' confrontation of philosophical belief with Revelation, he reaches the conclusion that the philosophical believer may acknowledge revealed faith "as a possible truth coming from other sources, even if he is unable to understand it." In fact, it is even possible to hold a "cousin's affection" for the one who believes in Revelation. Quite obviously there is a difference between, on the one hand, an existence only weakly related to transcendent reality by way of momentary imitations and symbols and, on the other hand, an existence which has really found access to transcendent reality by faith and which lives even now by virtue of that reality. And this *de facto* difference remains, as far as anthropological thought is concerned. However, at this point the question arises as to whether Jaspers considers it possible for man to manage with a transcendence which he can experience only in a "vanishing form," that is, whether man can accept such knowledge as definitive. If Jaspers sees man as a being that may not fix upon any truth, then it must follow that man may not be expected to fix upon Jaspers' own idea of man's

orientation to transcendent being. Clearly, then, it is
Jaspers' own thought which provides the very force which
will break this circle of existence impossible of fulfillment.
And the circle can open only in one direction: the fulfillment and completion of man's being as it is promised in
revelation.

Objective discussions, with non-Christian philosophers
invariably serve to confirm the fact that there are certain
points in non-Christian systems which find echo in revelation and which can be accepted by Christian thought.
This is true even of the militant atheism of the Marxist's
understanding of man. In proposing its world-oriented
expression of man's redemption, Marxism offers a "salvation history in the language of economic planning." By
the very fact that Marxism takes up the question of man's
salvation, a contact-point with Christianity is reached.
Despite the radical differences in the substantial content
of Christian and Marxist teachings, we can ask whether
the negative Marxist dogma—with its promises of worldly
salvation of man, with its promises of liberating man to
his true existence while simultaneously making him dependent upon society—does not, in fact, seek something
positive which it is unable to reach by its own devices and
which can be reached only in the Christian teaching
about man. Again, precisely in such teachings as are decidedly anti-faith do the points of contact with the true
faith prove to be quite distinct.

If, then, we may assume that even in those attempts to
solve the question of man that professedly oppose the

Christian answer are to be found contact points for the development of revealed truth, then we must next inquire into the ultimate reason for this. Is it simply a matter of historical fact that the separation from Christianity has not yet fully succeeded and that the new interpretations cannot, in fact, sift out the whole of the past? Such an explanation would not hold up even against the many recent attempts to explain man that are radically atheistic and declaredly anti-Christian. The answer must be sought in a fundamental principle about which the believer can be certain: that definition of man yielded from his having been created and redeemed by God and that image indelibly impressed in him from above still comes through even in the fragments and can still be detected in their broken forms. Just as splinters still suggest their belonging to a once integral whole, so also must the fragmentary projections of modern thought pay homage to their lost unity. The image of man shaped by Christian belief cannot be effaced. The presence of contact-points with non-Christian philosophies has been noted; now we see that the confrontation between the Christian and opposing views of man is anchored in a theological principle.

In light of the above, we find an explanation for the frequently observable agreement in certain problem-areas and motifs in thought about man, for example, the insight into the hopelessness of man left to himself and the striving to overcome this hopelessness. Here, especially, the basic notion of man's "being outside himself," the idea of his openness for the limitless and his inclination to transcendental reality, brings this thought into true proximity to biblical thought, even though this transcendental reality is often interpreted immanentistically and seldom is attainable. We may reasonably conclude from this that the biblical understanding of man is open to the questions of modern thought and is even able to provide real answers. Because modern thought, for the most part, goes no further than to pose the questions, theologian Paul Tillich had good reason for remarking that "existentialism has been a windfall for Christian theology." The assertion that existentialism offers Christian theology an exceptional opportunity to work out afresh and to prove the actuality and timeliness of the Christian answer to modern man's problems may also be made, with modification, of other modern attempts to interpret man to himself.

A true evaluation of the positive contact-points and trends in modern thinking about man will show that, in spite of specific and wide differences, they all fully agree on this: man is unfulfilled in his present state and seeks fulfillment in a higher state. In other words, they agree on modern man's awareness of being unredeemed and on his longing for redemption. If we now move on to determine precisely what these various systems mean by redemption, we shall discover a still further agreement among them. Man's fulfillment, they commonly hold, consists in that ideal existence in which man is fully himself and truly human, in which, having overcome his present incompleteness, he is able to transcend himself. This amounts to saying that man has a vague notion of a fulfillment in which he remains within himself and, at the same time, goes out beyond himself. Man reaches his completion, therefore, by the union of the human and meta-human; so unique is this joining of the two factors that the human is brought to itself only by the meta-human.

Regarding the question of whether such a dualism is possible and can bear fruit, we may well be skeptical with respect to unaided natural reason. Under the light of Revelation, however, it becomes clear that man's longing for that ideal existence, which is at once fully human and also something entirely new and meta-human, finds true fulfillment in the figure of the God-man as He has revealed Himself in faith. He is the secret center of unity and wholeness to which the splintered parts of the human image continue to refer. There is not only justification, but a very real need to effect the confrontation of the modern understanding of man with the Christian image of man as seen in the figure of the God-man. This does not mean a mere repetition of what we said earlier about the biblical conception of man and his orientation to Christ as seen in Holy Scripture. For that showed only how man can fully realize himself in exclusive relationship with Christ and in union with His life. In the confrontation of which we here speak, however, we shall endeavor to show that, even as the God-man, Christ realized this unity perfectly and consequently represents the image of fulfilled man in whom everything longed for and expressed by the most profound thinkers of a "post-Christian" age is also truly fulfilled.

D. THE GOD-MAN AS MAN'S ARCHETYPE AND NORM

There can be no doubt that everything which Revelation says about man has its focus in Jesus Christ and, therefore, that the figure of the God-man is the prototype and standard for judging man in general, even though the Scriptures do not express this truth in just so many words. To begin with, factual evidence shows that statements which the Bible makes about man find most perfect exemplification and fulfillment in Jesus Christ. Consider, for example, scriptural statements in the account of creation about man's likeness and proximity to God, about man's place as the lord of everything, about man's existing in a dialogue with God, about man's high stature and simultaneous lowliness in comparison with God, about man's unique calling and his tragedy. Everyone of these statements finds its highest meaning in the figure and fate of the God-man, Jesus Christ. And so, even in the Old Testament, Christ is the hidden center toward which all lines of thought run and which, in the New Testament, is fully revealed in the majesty, the dignity, and even in the self-elected lowliness of the Word become man.

Moreover, the Holy Scripture, especially the New Testament, also states literally that the God-man is the great goal of human strivings in general and that He is the standard against which everything human must be measured: "He is the image of the invisible God, the firstborn of every creature" (Colossians 1, 5); "To re-establish all things in Christ, both those in the heavens and those on the earth" (Ephesians 1, 10). Though this latter scriptural reference was written with special pertinence to Christ's Church, its meaning nonetheless extends to all humanity and to the world as His Body. And this means that every member of His Body, every single human being, is represented and possesses in Christ, its Head, an archetype and ideal; it means, further, that the members of His Body may truly be understood only in an understanding of the Head.

This biblical truth can be developed to the effect that the God-man, as the highest and most magnificent work of creation, was actually God's first purpose in His planning of the world of man, and that no human creature, standing under that Head, was called into existence except as dependent upon this highest purpose. At least, this is how the Church Fathers and a large array of theologians even to our day have explained this truth. Another expression of the same truth would be that the God-man was not made because of man, but rather humanity was made for, and modelled after, the God-man. Irenaeus of Lyons, for example, was able to say, and with great power: "Once the Redeemer was there, something had to be created which needed redemption, lest the God-man should be alone." Tertullian, writing about the formation of Adam from the clay of the earth, develops this thought still further: "That clay which God formed was already even then the image and likeness of the Christ who was to come in the flesh." Tertullian's statement also makes it clear that God had His eyes fixed upon the perfect man Jesus Christ as upon the ultimate goal of creation, so that all things else were instituted for His sake, all things are represented and epitomized in Him, and in light of Him all must be judged.

"The world [especially mankind] is a well-becoming entourage of the God-man" is the very graphic way in which Bernardine of Siena summed up what we have been saying here. In the God-man, human nature comes to meet us in its true and perfect form, that God-man who is the fullness of all that is human, the fullness from which every individual man draws his human substance. But if we now take this center and focus of all things human as the criterion according to which we shall judge the modern world's understanding of man, if we seek to determine whether the figure of the God-man still has meaning for the modern unresolved thinking about man, then we shall come immediately to two surprising observations. First of all, we shall observe that the transcendent tendency in modern thought—this reaching outside man for an extra-human reality and footing—is genuinely and legitimately human, and that the question posed by modern man here is a very real and legitimate one. Secondly, we shall see that the answer to this universal question is possible only from the vantage-point of

Christ. The figure of the God-man, therefore, can have a double effect in confronting modern thought. On the one hand, it can justify the whole question of transcendence and clarify the question better than the questioner himself is able to do; on the other, it provides an answer and can guarantee the attainment of transcendent reality, something which all modern immanentistic attempts have failed to do.

As man's perfect exemplar, the God-man is, at the same time, mankind's perfect model. The first decisive truth we derive from this perfect model is that human nature is not, in fact, something closed up into itself, that, positively, human nature is limitlessly open and oriented to something infinite. But this infinite is not a remote horizon that continuously withdraws as man advances, remaining permanently unattainable for man. No, the transcendent reality here is the personal God who has come in Christ out of absolute remoteness into a most intimately human nearness. The highest realization of man's nature in Jesus Christ makes clear that every man yearns for something divine and above man, yearns indeed, for union and oneness with God.

When Jesus Christ united humanity with the divine person, being God and man at the same time, he achieved such union in a unique and absolute way. This union between God and man cannot be repeated a second time. Two reasons militate against such an assumption. First another God-man could not be the head of entire humanity (human race). Secondly, it would be inconceivable that a divine person could be united to two independent human personalities. It follows that our union with God is of much lesser degree and intensity, and yet it is able to determine the characteristics of our human nature. The existence of the God-man reveals to us the innermost nature of our being human, our being's inner dependence on God, its relationship and even capability to participate in the divine life. The God-man, Jesus Christ, shows us that to be human means to be related to the eternal, absolute, and transcendental Good.

Yet it is important to understand this relationship not as something accidental to human nature. Being related to God has to be understood as an essential and integral element of the human spirit. To be human means to be open to the infinite in the way St. Thomas speaks of the human spirit when he claims that he is *"quodammodo omnia,"* that is infinite. If our assumption is correct, then all the strenuous efforts of the existentialists to gain for modern man an access to the transcendental can be seen in a new light. All these attempts can be understood as genuine desires of the human nature which was forever united to God in Christ Jesus. They are nothing but genuine manifestations of the human nature which is intrinsically related to God by grace and love. And only if we believe in the God-man can we fully understand Sartre's definition of man as a being who wants to become God.

Even the attempt of existentialism to establish a workable relationship with the transcendental can be fully understood only if we believe in Christ.

But the personality of Jesus Christ shows us also in what way this modern trend in the existentialistic philosophy goes astray. Despite all their efforts to relate man to the absolute and transcendental, they will not admit that man is capable of achieving such a destiny. Their exaggerated emphasis on an autonomous human nature makes them believe that such a nature, capable of a transcendental fulfillment, would not be a genuine nature. This is why Nietzsche came to the conclusion that God had to remain dead since a living God would be the "greatest obstacle to a genuine human existence." The existentialists, on the one hand, destroy human nature and, on the other hand, demand that modern man accept the tragedy with resignation. It is obvious that such a demand is senseless and against human dignity.

Man could not continue to exist in such a contradiction and state of tension. True, Christian thought also sets out from the conviction that man cannot fulfill and satisfy this striving after union with the divine *on his own power,* that he cannot realize his essence by himself. However, Christian thought does go on to say, with reference to the God-man, that this fulfillment comes from God and is manifest in the fact of the Incarnation. Hence the God-man clarifies for us not only the theoretical constitution and structure of man's nature as a relationship to God and a participation in His divine substance, but, even more, His Incarnation clarifies the fact that man's being can be satisfied and fulfilled by God alone. In the Incarnation it is not man who has risen up to God, but a divine person who has come down to humanity, raising man up to divinity. Thus the figure of the God-man is, at the same time, also the model for the way in which man can realize his existence, one which can be fulfilled by grace from God Himself. Man, oriented to participation in divine being, then becomes understandable at the same time as a being radically dependent upon the grace of God. For as much as human nature, because of its spirituality, yearns for the infinite, as much as it is able to reach out and to touch it, so to speak, the fact still remains that it cannot, by its own power, lay hold of and bring the divine down to the human. For that would be to give man power over the divine or to strip the divine of its true divinity—and this would mean depriving man of transcendental reality.

How superior the Christian answer is to all worldly conceptions of how man can be completed and redeemed is evident here again. Neither the self-sufficient, humanistic ethic of "Become what you are" nor the revolutionary passion of the Marxist self-redemption of man reach a goal that is really above man, because man obviously can attain with his powers only what is within those powers: man can never attain to anything that lies above himself. If man really wants to transcend himself, then he must do it by virtue of transcendent reality itself, and, where this truth is not understood, no striving by man for redemption and completion will ever be anything but a tragic fiction.

In this connection we may note that, remarkably enough, Christian and existentialist thinking actually coincide, if only momentarily. However, both come to totally opposed conclusions. The existentialist reacts by throwing man back on his own resources, locking him up all the more tightly in the straitjacket of his worldly existence. The Christian on the other hand, believes that man's extending himself after transcendent reality will be matched by God through His grace and that this has already reached its high-point in the Incarnation. At this point, the Christian way of thinking proves itself to be far superior to existentialist thought; it is precisely in its belief in the Incarnation and in grace coming down from above that it makes clear that man is not a faulty reality, that his existence is not like that of Sisyphus constantly rolling his stone uphill only to have it just as constantly roll back, thus making his task incessant. Christian thought understands man as a being always seeking God, always receiving a gracious hearing by God, always tending to completion through God.

Implied here is another more significant difference between the Christian and the existentialist understanding of man. It is the difference between the man, wholly and essentially dependent upon God, humbly open to grace and reverently attendant upon God, and that heroic superman who relies fully upon his own resources even when he knows he must fail. The relationship of Jesus with His Father in heaven is, of course, the model according to which man should stand in relation to God.

The grace of God is but another expression of that divine love which manifests itself as the truly creative force of God in man, as that power for growth which lets man mature to what God had, from the beginning, intended man to become. So perfectly revealed in Christ is this divine love that Christ was, even as man, the true and only Son of God. From this standpoint it becomes even clearer that man's incessant inclination toward God, his declared dependence upon God and his following of Christ really makes him a child and adoptive son of God.

This truth of the universal sonship of man to God can complete our picture of man in a significant way. Up to this point we concerned ourselves with the overwhelming greatness and awesome mysteriousness of this God-relatedness in man; we looked upon God in His unique majesty. Now, however, in view of man's filial relationship with God, divine majesty assumes the notes of fatherliness and warmth; stiffness and remoteness in divine-human relations give way before an intimacy which makes it possible for man to have an attitude of interior confidence and trust; and the rigid dialogue between the finite and the infinite becomes a conversation of love and warmth.

Neither the Marxist nor the existentialist, each with his defiant ethic of self-sufficiency and irreversible commitment to a tragic sense of life, will acknowledge as valid any such attitudes which characterize the Christian divine-human relationship as humility, sonship, or the intimacy of love. But it becomes clear how very pathetic, cramped, and frustrated is man's attitude as derived from modern non-Christian systems of thought. Here and there the existentialist even expresses the feeling that it is not at all unfitting for man to let himself be taken up and made whole by transcendent reality, and oftentimes impressions are given that passion for heroic self-sufficiency and the tragic recognition of the impossibility of fulfillment are unendurable. The impression is confirmed by statements suggesting expectancy, trust, and a childlike stance toward the absolute. One such instance is found in Heidegger who singles out our age alone as marked by "the absence of God," implying thereby the possibility of a new advent of God. Even in contemporary pessimistic literature we encounter similar reflections of human longing to be taken up by transcendent reality—the very human expectation of intervention by the absolute. Such reflections usually occur when the human need of love and the salvation of man through selfless love for others are regarded as real possibilities.

Of course, it has always been part of Christian thought that it is hardly unworthy of man to wait humbly upon the Absolute, to let oneself be taken up by something higher than himself, and to accept all this as a child. At the same time, as we noted earlier, the dynamic reality released by the God-man grips every human heart, whether it knows it or not. Clearly, there is a vast distance between the imperceptible burgeoning of this knowledge to the real acceptance of the grace of God in childlike humility. No small part of the difficulty faced by modern thought in traversing this distance is due to a misunderstanding occasioned by the day-to-day life of Christians in the world. Unfortunately, many non-Christian thinkers labor under the impression that Christians should face no real risks and hardships in life for the sole reason that they possess knowledge of being united with God; these thinkers seem to feel that this belief is sufficient to fulfill, satisfy, and stabilize human existence. Yet these modern thinkers see that this is not at all true in the lives of the Christians they observe. So what do these thinkers conclude? Simply this, that the Christian certitude of possessing God indicts the Christian as a visionary, possessing an unreal, unworkable answer to human living.

This indictment, a clarification of which is significant for us here, overlooks an important aspect of this union of the human and the divine in the Christian notion of man. A glance at such Old Testament figures as Job and the preachers should make clear that the accusation misses its mark when it expects human existence to find repose and security in being related to God. These figures show that a continuous dialogue with God always means danger for man in the sense that the demands of the speaking God generally place man in a state of violent tension which can be experienced only as insecurity, risk, suffering, and hardship.

This point also can be found in an exemplary way in the person of the God-man who, as man, knew no less insecurity and suffering than other men; in fact, the God-man experienced the distress and tragedy of human existence more deeply than other men because, as the man elevated by God, he reacted more sensitively to everything. For this reason we must not understand in any but the most real sense Christ's exclamation of abandonment on the cross (Mark 15, 34). That exclamation by the God-man is to be taken as the genuine expression of the deepest suffering humanly experienced by the God-man because His human nature was not yet glorified by His divine nature.

But if we ask why it is that man's union with God still leaves him in a typically earthly situation of tension, risk, hardship, and suffering, we shall find that it is not due only to the hiddenness of God or to the fact that our communion with God, because essentially based upon faith, cannot be seen and experienced as a full reality. It is due, on a deeper level, to the finiteness and weakness of created man in terms of which man must realize his spiritual being. The limited strength of a finite will means that, in the face of the high demands of God, man can fail in the details. It means that man's inclination toward the infinite can go to sleep, that he can fall down from the height on which he is placed because, as a being equipped only with limited strength, he never has himself firmly in his own hands. Since, on the side of man, union with God rests upon created and, therefore, limited power, it follows that man is fallible in his relations with God and that his being can "go wrong," and culpably so, in individual acts. The real state of the divine-human relationship is marked by the quality of finiteness and, therefore, man always lives with the possibility of actually falling from God and of being untrue to his decisions. This is already implied by the human make-up which must realize a relationship to the infinite in a finite way.

This constitution of man found its tragic expression in

the historical event of sin as a result of which man himself ruptured his original union with God. Ever since that event of original sin, the life of man is no longer determined only by creatural finiteness and fallibility, but also by fault and sin. It is these latter which place man's relations with God and his self-realization in the most serious crisis, threatening man with an absolute loss of his significance. Through His death on the cross, Christ eliminated this danger and settled the crisis. Christ's death on the cross, the most glorious act in the God-man's earthly life, fully clarifies what it means for man of a sin-scarred world to live his relationship to God and to realize himself. Such a relationship with God and such self-realization was possible for the God-man only through acceptance of the cross through which alone, according to the will of His Father, He could enter "into His glory" (Luke 24, 26). In a world burdened with sin and guilt, death on the cross was the means decreed by God for the glorification of the God-man, that is, for the completion of His relationship with the Father. At the same time, the realization of man's being on the cross was decreed as the way of transcending the world and rising to the divine. For the Christian, therefore, there is a realization of his relationship with God that is without tension, and man may transcend himself only through resistance to sin, only through a battle which can reach the point of total sacrifice of purely natural existence—in other words, through a battle which must be waged in the sign of the cross.

As a Christian existential reality, the cross means something more than the hopelessness in humanist thought, something more than the commitment of the Marxist to man's self-liberation. In both of these systems, struggle, commitment, and overcoming are nothing more than means of preserving that purely natural man who reaches growth by overcoming obstacles in the hope of attaining a deeper realization of his purely natural self. Diametrically opposed to this, the cross demands the relinquishing of the natural self even to the point of complete sacrifice of everything one has or is. Beyond this, suffering is, to the mind of both the existentialist and the Marxist, something that simply should not be, something intolerable, something which man may reject and inwardly refuse. The Christian, on the other hand, must love the cross as the divinely ordained opportunity for true self-transcendence, accepting it with a ready sacrificial spirit. We observe here the essential differences between a purely worldly understanding of existential difficulties and the Christian idea of the cross as the avenue to that supernatural human fulfillment. In noting these significant differences, we note also the absolute superiority of Christian sublimation of pain and suffering over any natural method for overcoming them. For only where suffering and pain are loved and voluntarily accepted in the light of the cross of Christ is human egoism really broken; there only is the way cleared for self-realization in orientation to the "total otherness" of divine life.

The Christian understanding of man as a limited being oriented to unlimited being but burdened with the cross, is obviously quite remote from viewing human existence as ideally a peaceful idyll with religious tones. As has been repeatedly explained by Christian existentialists (Kierkegaard, Peter Wust, and Gabriel Marcel), Christian thought does not spare man from the dangers and struggles encountered in human living. As a matter of fact, it would not be difficult to show that the existence of the God-oriented man is characterized by greater responsibility and need of decisiveness than the life of the man who neither knows of nor recognizes this divine-human relationship. Whoever does not regard eternity as his horizon, who knows nothing of the possibility of an eternal life and an eternal death cannot live by the life-and-death terms that always shape the Christian existence.

We reach a point in our study, particularly where we note our opposition to existentialism, where our vision suddenly appears to blur and where, perhaps, the Christian asks himself, in dismay, if his existence is not perhaps much unhappier than that erected on existentialist principles. Fundamentally, is the Christian in a worse position than the existentialist who depicts existence as surely unfulfilled and absurd, yet comes to terms with this unsuccessful existence untroubled by the possibility of an eternal failure? Such questioning demands that we always keep the whole of Christian teaching before us, above all that we keep in mind the divine plan and intention in creating man into an existence that, properly understood, is at once both limited and limitless. The meaning and purpose of such existence is unmistakably and entirely secure union with God; and for this the God-man is both example and archetype once more. There is the further meaning that acceptance of suffering and of crosses is both meaningful and, as it were, justifiable for the man convinced of the Christian idea. To the Christian, this acceptance finds vitality in a great hope; it makes all suffering—even sin, if it is overcome—fruitful and useful toward the acquisition of the completed form of man.

However, it is not merely hope for the future that fills and inspires the Christian, even in time of difficulty. Actually, for the God-oriented man, something of the fulfillment is already "pre-lived" in this hope. Why? Because in the willing acceptance and genuine living out of his God-related existence man experiences himself as God's partner and is conscious of having been called to a special dignity. Old Testament thought about man was conscious of this truth. Even if in the Old Testament it is the people of God *as a whole* which is understood as sharer in the Covenant and as in partnership with God, the implication remains steadfast that man, of all created beings, was chosen for dialogue with God. In the first account of creation in Genesis, only man is depicted as standing directly before God. Throughout Old Testament history there is no mistaking that man alone is called by God as partner in realizing divine plans. True, this is no partnership with equal rights; it is, nonetheless, a working and effective partnership in which the Lord of the Covenant keeps his absolute sovereignty at all times, man fulfilling his dependent function.

Only in the God-man did the divine-human partnership

attain full expression. The man Christ, personally united
with the second divine person, became the most perfect
instrument of divinity, the instrument which made it
possible for God to take personal part in the world actively. By utilizing this "instrument" in the decisive sal-
vation-process, God showed once and for all that He
wants and needs man as co-principle in the realization
of salvation, so that, to man, his own salvation will be
more meaningful by virtue of his own collaboration.

Some light on a basic tenet of the modern idea of man
is shed here. All modern attempts to explain man, even
though they set out from pessimistic beginnings, conclude with some form of activism. Sartre sees man's only
hope as lying in action. True, this might be regarded as
simply flight from the thoughtful consideration of human
reality into pure activity for its own sake, with the view
of making man forget his fundamental misery as effectively as possible. However, this is neither the meaning
nor the *raison d'être* of activism. In existentialism, for
example, activism is a consequence of the belief that man,
as being, is in no way fixed, that man is nothing but a
sketch to be filled in and polished with action. Man must
choose the self he is to become by action; thereby he
acquires his unique personal existence, even if it be an
existence condemned to failure. Man is what he actively
makes of himself, regardless of the final product.

This understanding of activism is part of the appeal to
so-called honesty and individuality by which is meant
that only what a person does alone and with his own

unaided resources is recognized as genuine and true. Man's autonomy, his own initiative and spontaneity are here elevated to absolutes. Yet, none of this understanding is rejected in the vision of man which we learn from Christ; on the contrary, it is both confirmed and even given a deeper foundation. In the God-man human activity and partnership with God was thwarted in no way; on the contrary, it was raised to its full effectiveness and power. Because the divinity in Christ did not remove the human, it therefore did not suppress or rob humanity of its autonomy and activity.

God always acts in such a way that created forces are never frustrated or extinguished, but raised to their true and full effectiveness. If it were otherwise, the dignity of creation would be infringed upon by its own Maker. And this is true regarding every man, even when we consider the difference between the hypostatic union in Christ and the union of other men with God. Again, grace does not extinguish man's collaboration, but actually calls upon it and gives it perfection.

Living in union with God, man is never dispensed from bringing his own full resources into play; rather, man is required to do so under an obligation of the highest order. Yet it never happens that man's autonomy is infringed upon by the sovereignty of God. God makes it possible for man to collaborate with God on his own. Such collaboration, though entirely man's own and the action of a true creature, is yet action by one who has acquired the dignity of being a partner of God.

Consequently, even the natural drive of man to realize himself and the world through action, a drive which marks the activism of modern man, finds its place in the Christian conception of man. Accordingly there are so many indications—and we could here have indicated many more—that the mystery of Christ, the archetype of all biblical thought about man, is also the mystery of man himself. The God-man proves to be the open sesame which opens for us the door to man, even to that man of our own day who has already lost himself or is in the process. On the question of man, Christ is "he who opens and no one shuts, who shuts and no one opens" (Apocalypse 3, 7). He is the key to that revelation which opens up the mystery of man. Apropos here is the maxim of Dostoyevski: "Never have I been able to picture man—without Him."

Selected Bibliography

Listed below, for reference, are the English editions of the principal works referred to in the course of this book.

Heinemann, Frederick, *Existentialism and the Modern Predicament* (New York: Harper and Row, 1958).

Benn, Gottfried, *Primal Vision, Selected Prose and Poetry* (New York: New Directions, 1960).

Scheler, Max, *Man's Place in Nature* (New York: Farrar, Strauss and Giroux, 1963).

——, *Philosophical Perspectives* (Boston: Beacon Press, 1958).

Brunner, H. Emil, *Christian Doctrine of God* (Philadelphia: Westminster Press, 1950).

Eichrodt, Walther, *Man in the Old Testament* (Naperville, Illinois: Alec R. Allenson, Inc., 1956).

Kohler, Ludwig, *Hebrew Man* (Nashville: Abingdon Press, 1957).

Stauffer, Ethelbert, *New Testament Theology* (New York: Macmillan Publishing Company).

Bultmann, Rudolf, *Theology of the New Testament* (New York: Charles Scribner's Sons).

———, *Primitive Christianity in Its Contemporary Setting* (Cleveland: World Publishing Company, 1956).

Westermann, Claus, *Essays on Old Testament Hermeneutics* (Richmond, Va.: John Knox Press, 1963).

———, *Genesis Accounts of Creation* (Philadelphia: Fortress Press, 1964).

———, *Praise of God in the Psalms* (Richmond, Va.: John Knox Press, 1965).

Engels, *see* Marx-Engels.

Marx, Karl, and Engels, Friedrich, *Basic Writings on Politics and Philosophy* (Magnolia, Mass.: Peter Smith Publisher).

———, *Capital* (International Publishers Company).

———, *Communist Manifesto* (New York: Russell and Russell, 1963).

Jaspers, Karl, *Future of Mankind* (Chicago: University of Chicago Press, 1963).

———, *Great Philosophers* (New York: Harcourt, Brace & World, Inc., 1962).

———, *Man in the Modern Age* (Garden City, N.Y.: Doubleday & Co., 1957).

———, *Nietzsche and Christianity* (Chicago: Henry Regnery, 1961).

———, *Reason and Existence* (New York: Farrar, Strauss and Giroux, 1957).

Heidegger, Martin, *Being and Time* (New York: Harper and Row Publishers, 1962).

———, *Existence and Being* (Chicago: Henry Regnery).

———, *Introduction to Metaphysics* (New York: Doubleday & Co.).

————, *What Is Philosophy?* (New York: Twayne Publishers).

Russell, Bertrand, *Why I Am Not a Christian* (New York: Simon & Schuster, Inc., 1962).

Hemingway, Ernest, *To Have and to Have Not* (New York: Charles Scribner's Sons, 1954).

————, *Farewell to Arms* (New York: Charles Scribner's Sons, 1923).

————, *Death in the Afternoon* (New York: Charles Scribner's Sons).

————, *For Whom the Bells Toll* (New York: Charles Scribner's Sons, 1940).

————, *The Sun Also Rises* (New York: Charles Scribner's Sons).

————, *The Old Man and the Sea* (New York: Charles Scribner's Sons).

Kafka, Franz, *Amerika* (New York: New Directions, 1962).

————, *The Castle* (New York: Alfred A. Knopf, Inc., 1954).

————, *The Trial* (New York: Alfred A. Knopf, Inc., 1957).

————, *Diaries,* 2 volumes (New York: Schocken Books, Inc., 1949).

Schoeps, H. J., *Jewish-Christian Argument* (New York: Holt, Rinehart and Winston, 1963).

————, *The Theology of the Apostles in the Light of Jewish Religious History* (Philadelphia: Westminster Press, 1961).

Wolfe, Thomas, *You Can't Go Home Again* (New York: Dell Publishing Company).

————, *Thomas Wolfe Reader* (New York: Charles Scribner's Sons, 1962).

Tillich, Paul, *Biblical Religion and the Search for the Ultimate Reality* (Chicago: University of Chicago Press, 1955).

————, *Systematic Theology* (Chicago: University of Chicago Press, 1957).

Nietzsche, Friedrich W., *Complete Works* (New York: Russell & Russell, Inc., 1964).